Americana

Student Workbook | Part 2

SpellingYouSee

Building Confidence

A Demme Learning Publication

Americana Student Workbook, Parts 1 and 2
©2014 Spelling You See
©2013 Karen J. Holinga, PhD.
Published and distributed by Demme Learning

www.SpellingYouSee.com

1-888-854-6284 or +1 717-283-1448 | www.demmelearning.com
Lancaster, Pennsylvania USA

ISBN 978-1-60826-611-1 (Americana Student Workbook)
ISBN 978-1-60826-613-5 (Part 2)
Revision Code 0816

Printed in the United States of America by Bindery Associates LLC

For information regarding CPSIA on this printed material call: 1-888-854-6284
and provide reference #0616-07272016

To the Instructor

This student book is the second half of Level D of Spelling You See. This innovative spelling program is designed to help your student become a confident and successful speller. The first few lessons will re-introduce the letter patterns the student learned in the *Americana Student Workbook, Part 1*. This is a good time to review the instructions and tips in your *Instructor's Handbook*.

1. Read the story to your student.

2. Read it together slowly. Have the student point to each word as you read.

3. Vowel chunks are two vowels that occur together in a word. They usually make one sound. Together with your student, find and mark all the **vowel chunks** in yellow.

George Washington Carver studied plants. He wanted to help farmers in the South. Raising cotton year after year had worn out the soil. He taught farmers to grow peanuts, sweet potatoes, and soybeans. These new crops helped build up the soil. They were also good for people to eat. Now the farmers could have better lives.

Vowel Chunks

aa	ae	ai	ao	au	aw	ay
ea	ee	ei	eo	ew	ey	eau
ia	ie	ii	io	iu		
oa	oe	oi	oo	ou	ow	oy
ua	ue	ui	uo	uy		

Copy the story and mark the vowel chunks. You may look at the opposite page if you need help.

George Washington Carver

G

studied plants. He wanted to

s

help farmers in the South.

h

Raising cotton year after year

R

had worn out the soil. He

h

taught farmers to grow

t

peanuts, sweet potatoes, and

P

soybeans.

s

1. Read the story to your student.

2. Read it together slowly. Have the student point to each word as you read.

3. Work with your student to find all the **vowel chunks** and mark them in yellow.

George Washington Carver studied plants. He wanted to help farmers in the South. Raising cotton year after year had worn out the soil. He taught farmers to grow peanuts, sweet potatoes, and soybeans. These new crops helped build up the soil. They were also good for people to eat. Now the farmers could have better lives.

Vowel Chunks

aa	ae	ai	ao	au	aw	ay
ea	ee	ei	eo	ew	ey	eau
ia	ie	ii	io	iu		
oa	oe	oi	oo	ou	ow	oy
ua	ue	ui	uo	uy		

Copy and "chunk" the story by marking the vowel chunks. You may look at the opposite page if you need help.

He taught farmers to grow

H

peanuts, sweet potatoes, and

P

soybeans. These new crops

s

helped build up the soil. They

h

were also good for people to

w

eat. Now the farmers could

e

have better lives.

h

1. Read the story to your student.
2. Read it together slowly. Have the student point to each word as you read.
3. Together, find all the <u>vowel chunks</u> in the passage and mark them in yellow.

George Washington Carver studied plants. He wanted to help farmers in the South. Raising cotton year after year had worn out the soil. He taught farmers to grow peanuts, sweet potatoes, and soybeans. These new crops helped build up the soil. They were also good for people to eat. Now the farmers could have better lives.

Vowel Chunks

aa	ae	ai	ao	au	aw	ay
ea	ee	ei	eo	ew	ey	eau
ia	ie	ii	io	iu		
oa	oe	oi	oo	ou	ow	oy
ua	ue	ui	uo	uy		

Copy and chunk the story by marking the vowel chunks. You may look at the opposite page if you need help.

George Washington Carver

G

studied plants. He wanted to

s

help farmers in the South.

h

Raising cotton year after year

R

had worn out the soil. He

h

taught farmers to grow

t

peanuts, sweet potatoes, and

P

soybeans.

s

1. Read the story to your student.

2. Read it together slowly. Have the student point to each word as you read.

3. Together, find all the <u>vowel chunks</u> in the passage and mark them in yellow.

4. All the passages in this workbook are also in the back of the *Instructor's Handbook* under **Resources**. When dictating the passage, you may want to cover this page with a piece of paper and read the story from the *Handbook*.

George Washington Carver studied plants. He wanted to help farmers in the South. Raising cotton year after year had worn out the soil. He taught farmers to grow peanuts, sweet potatoes, and soybeans. These new crops helped build up the soil. They were also good for people to eat. Now the farmers could have better lives.

Vowel Chunks

aa	ae	ai	ao	au	aw	ay
ea	ee	ei	eo	ew	ey	eau
ia	ie	ii	io	iu		
oa	oe	oi	oo	ou	ow	oy
ua	ue	ui	uo	uy		

Write this week's story from dictation. Ask for help if you need it.

George

1. Read the story to your student.

2. Read it together slowly. Have the student point to each word as you read.

3. Together, find all the <u>vowel chunks</u> in the passage and mark them in yellow.

George Washington Carver studied plants. He wanted to help farmers in the South. Raising cotton year after year had worn out the soil. He taught farmers to grow peanuts, sweet potatoes, and soybeans. These new crops helped build up the soil. They were also good for people to eat. Now the farmers could have better lives.

Vowel Chunks

aa	ae	ai	ao	au	aw	ay
ea	ee	ei	eo	ew	ey	eau
ia	ie	ii	io	iu		
oa	oe	oi	oo	ou	ow	oy
ua	ue	ui	uo	uy		

Section 2: Second Dictation

See if you can write this week's story from dictation without asking for help.

20A

1. Read the story to your student.

2. Read it together slowly. Have the student point to each word as you read.

3. Help your student look for and mark all the <u>**consonant chunks**</u> in blue. Some consonant chunks may be silent or change sounds completely.

Rosa Parks had worked a long day. She got on the bus and dropped into a seat. Soon a white man got on the bus. Rosa was African American. Since the seats for white people were all full, the driver ordered Rosa to move back. That day Rosa decided not to move. It seemed wrong to her. When she did not move, she was arrested.

Consonant Chunks

ch	gh	ph	sh	th	wh
gn	kn	qu	wr	dg	ck	tch
bb	cc	dd	ff	gg	hh	kk	ll	mm
nn	pp	rr	ss	tt	ww	vv	zz

Copy and chunk the story by marking the consonant chunks. You may look at the opposite page if you need help.

Rosa Parks had worked a long

R

day. She got on the bus and

d

dropped into a seat. Soon a

d

white man got on the bus.

w

Rosa was African American.

R

Since the seats for white

S

people were all full, the driver

P

ordered Rosa to move back.

O

20B

1. Read the story to your student.

2. Read it together slowly. Have the student point to each word as you read.

3. Help your student look for and mark all the <u>**consonant chunks**</u> in blue.

Rosa Parks had worked a long day. She got on the bus and dropped into a seat. Soon a white man got on the bus. Rosa was African American. Since the seats for white people were all full, the driver ordered Rosa to move back. That day Rosa decided not to move. It seemed wrong to her. When she did not move, she was arrested.

Consonant Chunks

ch	gh	ph	sh	th	wh
gn	kn	qu	wr	dg	ck	tch
bb	cc	dd	ff	gg	hh	kk	ll	mm
nn	pp	rr	ss	tt	ww	vv	zz

Copy and chunk the story by marking the consonant chunks. You may look at the opposite page if you need help.

Since the seats for white

S

people were all full, the driver

P

ordered Rosa to move back.

o

That day Rosa decided not to

T

move. It seemed wrong to her.

m

When she did not move, she

W

was arrested.

W

20C

1. Read the story to your student.
2. Read it together slowly. Have the student point to each word as you read.
3. Help your student look for and mark all the <u>**consonant chunks**</u> in blue.

Rosa Parks had worked a long day. She got on the bus and dropped into a seat. Soon a white man got on the bus. Rosa was African American. Since the seats for white people were all full, the driver ordered Rosa to move back. That day Rosa decided not to move. It seemed wrong to her. When she did not move, she was arrested.

Consonant Chunks

ch	gh	ph	sh	th	wh		
gn	kn	qu	wr	dg	ck	tch	
bb	cc	dd	ff	gg	hh	kk	ll	mm
nn	pp	rr	ss	tt	ww	vv	zz

Copy and chunk the story by marking the consonant chunks. You may look at the opposite page if you need help.

Rosa Parks had worked a long

R

day. She got on the bus and

d

dropped into a seat. Soon a

d

white man got on the bus.

w

Rosa was African American.

R

Since the seats for white

S

people were all full, the driver

P

ordered Rosa to move back.

o

1. Read the story to your student.

2. Read it together slowly. Have the student point to each word as you read.

3. Together, find all the <u>consonant chunks</u> in the passage and mark them in blue.

Rosa Parks had worked a long day. She got on the bus and dropped into a seat. Soon a white man got on the bus. Rosa was African American. Since the seats for white people were all full, the driver ordered Rosa to move back. That day Rosa decided not to move. It seemed wrong to her. When she did not move, she was arrested.

Consonant Chunks

ch	gh	ph	sh	th	wh		
gn	kn	qu	wr	dg	ck	tch	
bb	cc	dd	ff	gg	hh	kk	ll	mm
nn	pp	rr	ss	tt	ww	vv	zz

Write this week's story from dictation. Ask for help if you need it.

Rosa

1. Read the story to your student.

2. Read it together slowly. Have the student point to each word as you read.

3. Together, find all the <u>consonant chunks</u> in the passage and mark them in blue.

Rosa Parks had worked a long day. She got on the bus and dropped into a seat. Soon a white man got on the bus. Rosa was African American. Since the seats for white people were all full, the driver ordered Rosa to move back. That day Rosa decided not to move. It seemed wrong to her. When she did not move, she was arrested.

Consonant Chunks
ch	gh	ph	sh	th	wh
gn	kn	qu	wr	dg	ck	tch
bb	cc	dd	ff	gg	hh	kk	ll	mm
nn	pp	rr	ss	tt	ww	vv	zz

Section 2: Second Dictation

See if you can write this week's story from dictation without asking for help.

1. Read the story to your student.

2. Read it together slowly. Have the student point to each word as you read.

3. Together, find and mark all the **vowel chunks** and **consonant chunks**. Use yellow for <u>**vowel chunks**</u> and blue for <u>**consonant chunks**</u>.

When Martin was six, his closest friend was ordered not to play with him. It was because Martin was African American. Martin didn't understand. His parents assured him that he was as good as anyone else. In 1963 Martin Luther King, Junior gave a speech. He said, "I have a dream." He dreamed people would be judged by what they do and say, not by their skin color.

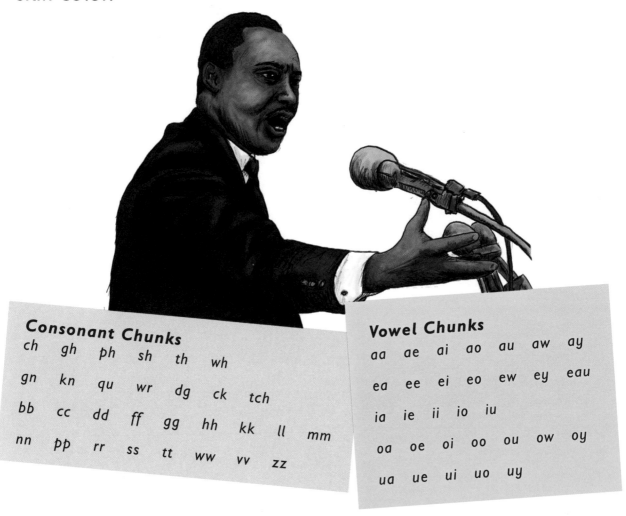

Consonant Chunks

ch	gh	ph	sh	th	wh			
gn	kn	qu	wr	dg	ck	tch		
bb	cc	dd	ff	gg	hh	kk	ll	mm
nn	pp	rr	ss	tt	ww	vv	zz	

Vowel Chunks

aa	ae	ai	ao	au	aw	ay
ea	ee	ei	eo	ew	ey	eau
ia	ie	ii	io	iu		
oa	oe	oi	oo	ou	ow	oy
ua	ue	ui	uo	uy		

Copy and chunk the story by marking the vowel chunks and consonant chunks.
You may look at the opposite page if you need help.

When Martin was six, his

W

closest friend was ordered not

c

to play with him. It was

t

because Martin was African

b

American. Martin didn't

A

understand. His parents assured

u

him that he was as good as

h

anyone else.

a

1. Read the story to your student.

2. Read it together slowly. Have the student point to each word as you read.

3. Together, find and mark all the **vowel chunks** and **consonant chunks**. Use yellow for <u>vowel chunks</u> and blue for <u>consonant chunks</u>.

When Martin was six, his closest friend was ordered not to play with him. It was because Martin was African American. Martin didn't understand. His parents assured him that he was as good as anyone else. In 1963 Martin Luther King, Junior gave a speech. He said, "I have a dream." He dreamed people would be judged by what they do and say, not by their skin color.

Consonant Chunks

ch	gh	ph	sh	th	wh		
gn	kn	qu	wr	dg	ck	tch	
bb	cc	dd	ff	gg	hh	kk	ll	mm
nn	pp	rr	ss	tt	ww	vv	zz	

Vowel Chunks

aa	ae	ai	ao	au	aw	ay
ea	ee	ei	eo	ew	ey	eau
ia	ie	ii	io	iu		
oa	oe	oi	oo	ou	ow	oy
ua	ue	ui	uo	uy		

Copy and chunk the story by marking the vowel chunks and consonant chunks. You may look at the opposite page if you need help.

His parents assured him that

H

he was as good as anyone

h

else. In 1963 Martin Luther

e

King, Junior gave a speech.

K

He said, "I have a dream."

H

He dreamed people would be

H

judged by what they do and

j

say, not by their skin color.

S

1. Read the story to your student.

2. Read it together slowly. Have the student point to each word as you read.

3. Together, find and mark all the **vowel chunks** and **consonant chunks**. Use yellow for <u>**vowel chunks**</u> and blue for <u>**consonant chunks**</u>.

When Martin was six, his closest friend was ordered not to play with him. It was because Martin was African American. Martin didn't understand. His parents assured him that he was as good as anyone else. In 1963 Martin Luther King, Junior gave a speech. He said, "I have a dream." He dreamed people would be judged by what they do and say, not by their skin color.

Consonant Chunks

ch	gh	ph	sh	th	wh			
gn	kn	qu	wr	dg	ck	tch		
bb	cc	dd	ff	gg	hh	kk	ll	mm
nn	pp	rr	ss	tt	ww	vv	zz	

Vowel Chunks

aa	ae	ai	ao	au	aw	ay
ea	ee	ei	eo	ew	ey	eau
ia	ie	ii	io	iu		
oa	oe	oi	oo	ou	ow	oy
ua	ue	ui	uo	uy		

Copy and chunk the story by marking the vowel chunks and consonant chunks.
You may look at the opposite page if you need help.

When Martin was six, his

W

closest friend was ordered not

c

to play with him. It was

t

because Martin was African

b

American. Martin didn't

A

understand. His parents assured

u

him that he was as good as

h

anyone else.

a

1. Read the story to your student.

2. Read it together slowly. Have the student point to each word as you read.

3. Together, find and mark all the **vowel chunks** and **consonant chunks**. Use yellow for <u>**vowel chunks**</u> and blue for <u>**consonant chunks**</u>.

When Martin was six, his closest friend was ordered not to play with him. It was because Martin was African American. Martin didn't understand. His parents assured him that he was as good as anyone else. In 1963 Martin Luther King, Junior gave a speech. He said, "I have a dream." He dreamed people would be judged by what they do and say, not by their skin color.

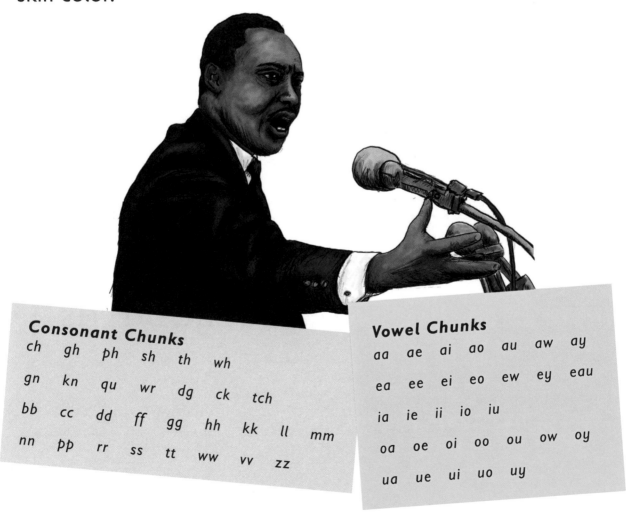

Consonant Chunks

ch	gh	ph	sh	th	wh	
gn	kn	qu	wr	dg	ck	tch
bb	cc	dd	ff	gg	hh	kk	ll	mm
nn	pp	rr	ss	tt	ww	vv	zz

Vowel Chunks

aa	ae	ai	ao	au	aw	ay
ea	ee	ei	eo	ew	ey	eau
ia	ie	ii	io	iu		
oa	oe	oi	oo	ou	ow	oy
ua	ue	ui	uo	uy		

Section 2: First Dictation

Write this week's story from dictation. Ask for help if you need it.

When

1. Read the story to your student.

2. Read it together slowly. Have the student point to each word as you read.

3. Together, find and mark all the **vowel chunks** and **consonant chunks**. Use yellow for **vowel chunks** and blue for **consonant chunks**.

When Martin was six, his closest friend was ordered not to play with him. It was because Martin was African American. Martin didn't understand. His parents assured him that he was as good as anyone else. In 1963 Martin Luther King, Junior gave a speech. He said, "I have a dream." He dreamed people would be judged by what they do and say, not by their skin color.

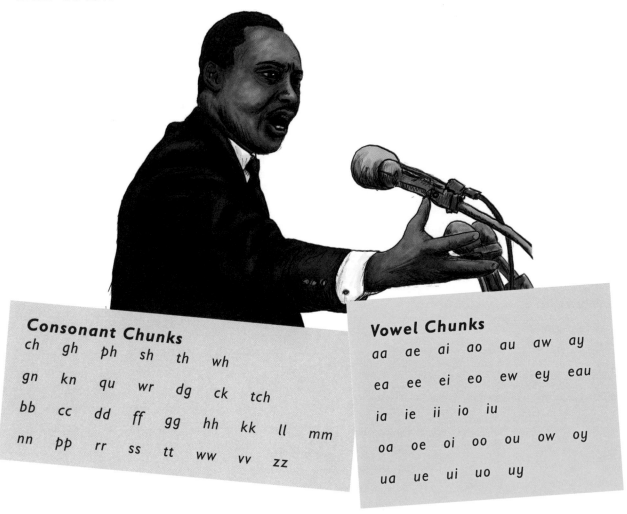

Consonant Chunks

ch gh ph sh th wh

gn kn qu wr dg ck tch

bb cc dd ff gg hh kk ll mm

nn pp rr ss tt ww vv zz

Vowel Chunks

aa ae ai ao au aw ay

ea ee ei eo ew ey eau

ia ie ii io iu

oa oe oi oo ou ow oy

ua ue ui uo uy

See if you can write this week's story from dictation without asking for help.

I spelled _____ words correctly.

1. Read the story to your student.

2. Read it together slowly. Have the student point to each word as you read.

3. The letter *r* often changes or "bosses" the sound of the vowel it follows. Together, look for **Bossy *r* chunks** and mark them in purple.

When Lincoln was president, he signed the Homestead Act. A person could own 160 acres after moving to the land, building a home, and farming for five years. On the plains, settlers built their homes from sod. Winters were freezing. Summers were dry. Insects ate crops. There were storms and tornadoes. The settlers worked hard because they wanted their own land.

Bossy r Chunks
ar   er   ir   or   ur

Copy the story. Mark all the Bossy *r* chunks on your copy.

When Lincoln was president,

W

he signed the Homestead Act.

h

A person could own 160 acres

A

after moving to the land,

a

building a home, and farming

b

for five years. On the plains,

f

settlers built their homes

s

from sod.

f

1. Read the story to your student.

2. Read it together slowly. Have the student point to each word as you read.

3. Help your student find and mark the **Bossy *r* chunks** in purple.

When Lincoln was president, he signed the Homestead Act.
A person could own 160 acres after moving to the land, building
a home, and farming for five years. On the plains, settlers
built their homes from sod. Winters were freezing. Summers
were dry. Insects ate crops. There were storms and tornadoes.
The settlers worked hard because they wanted their own land.

Bossy r Chunks
ar   er   ir   or   ur

Copy the story. Mark all the Bossy *r* chunks on your copy.

On the plains, settlers built

o

their homes from sod. Winters

t

were freezing. Summers were

w

dry. Insects ate crops. There

d

were storms and tornadoes. The

w

settlers worked hard because

s

they wanted their own land.

t

1. Read the story to your student.

2. Read it together slowly. Have the student point to each word as you read.

3. Help your student find and mark the **Bossy _r_ chunks** in purple.

When Lincoln was president, he signed the Homestead Act. A person could own 160 acres after moving to the land, building a home, and farming for five years. On the plains, settlers built their homes from sod. Winters were freezing. Summers were dry. Insects ate crops. There were storms and tornadoes. The settlers worked hard because they wanted their own land.

Bossy r Chunks
ar   er   ir   or   ur

Copy the story. Mark all the Bossy *r* chunks on your copy.

When Lincoln was president,

W

he signed the Homestead Act.

h

A person could own 160 acres

A

after moving to the land,

a

building a home, and farming

b

for five years. On the plains,

f

settlers built their homes

s

from sod.

f

1. Read the story to your student.

2. Read it together slowly. Have the student point to each word as you read.

3. Help your student find and mark the **Bossy _r_ chunks** in purple.

When Lincoln was president, he signed the Homestead Act. A person could own 160 acres after moving to the land, building a home, and farming for five years. On the plains, settlers built their homes from sod. Winters were freezing. Summers were dry. Insects ate crops. There were storms and tornadoes. The settlers worked hard because they wanted their own land.

Bossy r Chunks
ar   er   ir   or   ur

Write this week's story from dictation. Ask for help if you need it.

When

1. Read the story to your student.

2. Read it together slowly. Have the student point to each word as you read.

3. Help your student find and mark the <u>**Bossy *r* chunks**</u> in purple.

When Lincoln was president, he signed the Homestead Act. A person could own 160 acres after moving to the land, building a home, and farming for five years. On the plains, settlers built their homes from sod. Winters were freezing. Summers were dry. Insects ate crops. There were storms and tornadoes. The settlers worked hard because they wanted their own land.

Bossy r Chunks
ar   er   ir   or   ur

Section 2: Second Dictation

See if you can write this week's story from dictation without asking for help.

1. Read the story to your student.

2. Read it together slowly. Have the student point to each word as you read.

3. This week, look for all three letter patterns you have just reviewed. Mark **vowel chunks** in yellow, **consonant chunks** in blue, and **Bossy *r* chunks** in purple.

New settlers kept arriving in the colonies, but the best farmland was already owned. People needed to move west to find places to live. Daniel Boone and his family were some of the first settlers to move to Kentucky. Daniel was a hunter and trapper. He spent much of his time in the forest. He was hired to cut a new road into Kentucky. Now more settlers could move there using the Wilderness Road.

Consonant Chunks

ch gh ph sh th wh
gn kn qu wr dg ck tch
bb cc dd ff gg hh kk ll mm
nn pp rr ss tt ww vv zz

Bossy r Chunks

ar er ir or ur

Vowel Chunks

aa ae ai ao au aw ay
ea ee ei eo ew ey eau
ia ie ii io iu
oa oe oi oo ou ow oy
ua ue ui uo uy

Copy and chunk the story by marking the vowel chunks, consonant chunks, and Bossy *r* chunks.

New settlers kept arriving in

N

the colonies, but the best

t

farmland was already owned.

f

People needed to move west

P

to find places to live. Daniel

t

Boone and his family were

B

some of the first settlers to

s

move to Kentucky.

m

1. Read the story to your student.

2. Read it together slowly. Have the student point to each word as you read.

3. Together, mark **vowel chunks** in yellow, **consonant chunks** in blue, and **Bossy *r* chunks** in purple.

New settlers kept arriving in the colonies, but the best farmland was already owned. People needed to move west to find places to live. Daniel Boone and his family were some of the first settlers to move to Kentucky. Daniel was a hunter and trapper. He spent much of his time in the forest. He was hired to cut a new road into Kentucky. Now more settlers could move there using the Wilderness Road.

Consonant Chunks

ch   gh   ph   sh   th   wh
gn   kn   qu   wr   dg   ck   tch
bb   cc   dd   ff   gg   hh   kk   ll   mm
nn   pp   rr   ss   tt   ww   vv   zz

Bossy r Chunks

ar   er   ir   or   ur

Vowel Chunks

aa   ae   ai   ao   au   aw   ay
ea   ee   ei   eo   ew   ey   eau
ia   ie   ii   io   iu
oa   oe   oi   oo   ou   ow   oy
ua   ue   ui   uo   uy

Copy and chunk the story by marking the vowel chunks, consonant chunks, and Bossy *r* chunks.

Daniel was a hunter and

D

trapper. He spent much of his

t

time in the forest. He was

t

hired to cut a new road into

h

Kentucky. Now more settlers

K

could move there using the

c

Wilderness Road.

W

1. Read the story to your student.

2. Read it together slowly. Have the student point to each word as you read.

3. Together, mark <u>**vowel chunks**</u> in yellow, <u>**consonant chunks**</u> in blue, and <u>**Bossy *r* chunks**</u> in purple.

New settlers kept arriving in the colonies, but the best farmland was already owned. People needed to move west to find places to live. Daniel Boone and his family were some of the first settlers to move to Kentucky. Daniel was a hunter and trapper. He spent much of his time in the forest. He was hired to cut a new road into Kentucky. Now more settlers could move there using the Wilderness Road.

Consonant Chunks

ch	gh	ph	sh	th	wh			
gn	kn	qu	wr	dg	ck	tch		
bb	cc	dd	ff	gg	hh	kk	ll	mm
nn	pp	rr	ss	tt	ww	vv	zz	

Bossy r Chunks

ar	er	ir	or	ur

Vowel Chunks

aa	ae	ai	ao	au	aw	ay
ea	ee	ei	eo	ew	ey	eau
ia	ie	ii	io	iu		
oa	oe	oi	oo	ou	ow	oy
ua	ue	ui	uo	uy		

Copy and chunk the story by marking the vowel chunks, consonant chunks, and Bossy *r* chunks.

New settlers kept arriving in

N

the colonies, but the best

t

farmland was already owned.

f

People needed to move west

P

to find places to live. Daniel

t

Boone and his family were

B

some of the first settlers to

s

move to Kentucky.

m

1. Read the story to your student.

2. Read it together slowly. Have the student point to each word as you read.

3. Together, mark **vowel chunks** in yellow, **consonant chunks** in blue, and **Bossy *r* chunks** in purple.

New settlers kept arriving in the colonies, but the best farmland was already owned. People needed to move west to find places to live. Daniel Boone and his family were some of the first settlers to move to Kentucky. Daniel was a hunter and trapper. He spent much of his time in the forest. He was hired to cut a new road into Kentucky. Now more settlers could move there using the Wilderness Road.

Consonant Chunks

ch	gh	ph	sh	th	wh
gn	kn	qu	wr	dg	ck	tch
bb	cc	dd	ff	gg	hh	kk	ll	mm
nn	pp	rr	ss	tt	ww	vv	zz

Bossy r Chunks

ar er ir or ur

Vowel Chunks

aa	ae	ai	ao	au	aw	ay
ea	ee	ei	eo	ew	ey	eau
ia	ie	ii	io	iu
oa	oe	oi	oo	ou	ow	oy
ua	ue	ui	uo	uy

Section 2: First Dictation

Write this week's story from dictation. Ask for help if you need it.

New

I spelled _____ words correctly.

23E

1. Read the story to your student.

2. Read it together slowly. Have the student point to each word as you read.

3. Together, mark **vowel chunks** in yellow, **consonant chunks** in blue, and **Bossy *r* chunks** in purple.

New settlers kept arriving in the colonies, but the best farmland was already owned. People needed to move west to find places to live. Daniel Boone and his family were some of the first settlers to move to Kentucky. Daniel was a hunter and trapper. He spent much of his time in the forest. He was hired to cut a new road into Kentucky. Now more settlers could move there using the Wilderness Road.

Consonant Chunks

ch gh ph sh th wh
gn kn qu wr dg ck tch
bb cc dd ff gg hh kk ll mm
nn pp rr ss tt ww vv zz

Bossy r Chunks

ar er ir or ur

Vowel Chunks

aa ae ai ao au aw ay
ea ee ei eo ew ey eau
ia ie ii io iu
oa oe oi oo ou ow oy
ua ue ui uo uy

Section 2: Second Dictation

See if you can write this week's story from dictation without asking for help.

I spelled _____ words correctly.

1. Read the story to your student.

2. Read it together slowly. Have the student point to each word as you read.

3. Together, mark the <u>vowel chunks</u>, <u>consonant chunks</u>, and **<u>Bossy r chunks</u>**. Be sure to use the correct color for each letter pattern. See the *Handbook* for tips on marking overlapping chunks.

Davy Crockett wrote, "Be sure you're right; then go ahead." That's how he thought, and that's how he lived. Davy was born in Tennessee. Over the years he had many jobs. After getting married, he was a farmer. Then he was an army officer. He even served in the United States Congress. After that, Davy went to help Texas become free from Mexico. He fought and died in Texas at a place called the Alamo.

Consonant Chunks

ch	gh	ph	sh	th	wh		
gn	kn	qu	wr	dg	ck	tch	
bb	cc	dd	ff	gg	hh	kk	ll	mm
nn	pp	rr	ss	tt	ww	vv	zz

Bossy r Chunks

ar   er   ir   or   ur

Vowel Chunks

aa	ae	ai	ao	au	aw	ay
ea	ee	ei	eo	ew	ey	eau
ia	ie	ii	io	iu		
oa	oe	oi	oo	ou	ow	oy
ua	ue	ui	uo	uy		

Copy and chunk the story by marking the vowel chunks, consonant chunks, and Bossy *r* chunks.

Davy Crockett wrote, "Be sure

D

you're right; then go ahead."

y

That's how he thought, and

T

that's how he lived. Davy was

t

born in Tennessee. Over the

b

years he had many jobs. After

y

getting married, he was a

g

farmer.

f

1. Read the story to your student.

2. Read it together slowly. Have the student point to each word as you read.

3. Together, mark the <u>**vowel chunks**</u>, <u>**consonant chunks**</u>, and <u>**Bossy *r* chunks**</u>. Be sure to use the correct color for each letter pattern.

Davy Crockett wrote, "Be sure you're right; then go ahead." That's how he thought, and that's how he lived. Davy was born in Tennessee. Over the years he had many jobs. After getting married, he was a farmer. Then he was an army officer. He even served in the United States Congress. After that, Davy went to help Texas become free from Mexico. He fought and died in Texas at a place called the Alamo.

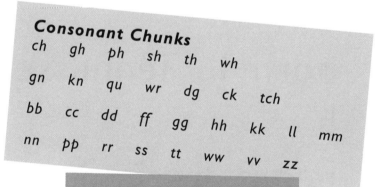

Consonant Chunks

ch   gh   ph   sh   th   wh

gn   kn   qu   wr   dg   ck   tch

bb   cc   dd   ff   gg   hh   kk   ll   mm

nn   pp   rr   ss   tt   ww   vv   zz

Bossy r Chunks

ar   er   ir   or   ur

Vowel Chunks

aa   ae   ai   ao   au   aw   ay

ea   ee   ei   eo   ew   ey   eau

ia   ie   ii   io   iu

oa   oe   oi   oo   ou   ow   oy

ua   ue   ui   uo   uy

Copy and chunk the story by marking the vowel chunks, consonant chunks, and Bossy *r* chunks.

After getting married, he was
A

a farmer. Then he was an army
a

officer. He even served in the
o

United States Congress. After
U

that, Davy went to help Texas
t

become free from Mexico. He
b

fought and died in Texas at a
f

place called the Alamo.
P

1. Read the story to your student.

2. Read it together slowly. Have the student point to each word as you read.

3. Together, mark the <u>vowel chunks</u>, <u>consonant chunks</u>, and <u>**Bossy *r* chunks**</u>. Be sure to use the correct color for each letter pattern.

Davy Crockett wrote, "Be sure you're right; then go ahead." That's how he thought, and that's how he lived. Davy was born in Tennessee. Over the years he had many jobs. After getting married, he was a farmer. Then he was an army officer. He even served in the United States Congress. After that, Davy went to help Texas become free from Mexico. He fought and died in Texas at a place called the Alamo.

Consonant Chunks

ch gh ph sh th wh
gn kn qu wr dg ck tch
bb cc dd ff gg hh kk ll mm
nn pp rr ss tt ww vv zz

Bossy r Chunks

ar er ir or ur

Vowel Chunks

aa ae ai ao au aw ay
ea ee ei eo ew ey eau
ia ie ii io iu
oa oe oi oo ou ow oy
ua ue ui uo uy

Copy and chunk the story by marking the vowel chunks, consonant chunks, and Bossy *r* chunks.

Davy Crockett wrote, "Be sure

D

you're right; then go ahead."

y

That's how he thought, and

T

that's how he lived. Davy was

t

born in Tennessee. Over the

b

years he had many jobs. After

y

getting married, he was a

g

farmer.

f

1. Read the story to your student.

2. Read it together slowly. Have the student point to each word as you read.

3. Together, mark the <u>**vowel chunks**</u>, <u>**consonant chunks**</u>, and <u>**Bossy *r* chunks**</u>. Be sure to use the correct color for each letter pattern.

Davy Crockett wrote, "Be sure you're right; then go ahead." That's how he thought, and that's how he lived. Davy was born in Tennessee. Over the years he had many jobs. After getting married, he was a farmer. Then he was an army officer. He even served in the United States Congress. After that, Davy went to help Texas become free from Mexico. He fought and died in Texas at a place called the Alamo.

Consonant Chunks

ch   gh   ph   sh   th   wh
gn   kn   qu   wr   dg   ck   tch
bb   cc   dd   ff   gg   hh   kk   ll   mm
nn   pp   rr   ss   tt   ww   vv   zz

Bossy r Chunks

ar   er   ir   or   ur

Vowel Chunks

aa   ae   ai   ao   au   aw   ay
ea   ee   ei   eo   ew   ey   eau
ia   ie   ii   io   iu
oa   oe   oi   oo   ou   ow   oy
ua   ue   ui   uo   uy

Section 2: First Dictation

Write this week's story from dictation. Ask for help if you need it.

Davy

1. Read the story to your student.

2. Read it together slowly. Have the student point to each word as you read.

3. Together, mark the **vowel chunks**, **consonant chunks**, and **Bossy *r* chunks**. Be sure to use the correct color for each letter pattern.

Davy Crockett wrote, "Be sure you're right; then go ahead." That's how he thought, and that's how he lived. Davy was born in Tennessee. Over the years he had many jobs. After getting married, he was a farmer. Then he was an army officer. He even served in the United States Congress. After that, Davy went to help Texas become free from Mexico. He fought and died in Texas at a place called the Alamo.

Consonant Chunks

ch	gh	ph	sh	th	wh		
gn	kn	qu	wr	dg	ck	tch	
bb	cc	dd	ff	gg	hh	kk	ll	mm
nn	pp	rr	ss	tt	ww	vv	zz

Bossy r Chunks

ar er ir or ur

Vowel Chunks

aa	ae	ai	ao	au	aw	ay
ea	ee	ei	eo	ew	ey	eau
ia	ie	ii	io	iu		
oa	oe	oi	oo	ou	ow	oy
ua	ue	ui	uo	uy		

Section 2: Second Dictation

See if you can write this week's story from dictation without asking for help.

1. Read the story to your student.

2. Read it together slowly. Have the student point to each word as you read.

3. Some words have silent letters that are not part of other chunks. In this lesson, look for silent *e* and silent *l*. Always mark **silent letters** in orange.

Imagine you were moving far away and could take only one plaything. What would you take? Pioneer children had to make this choice. They might choose a book or a doll. Families were supposed to pack only what was needed. The wagons were filled with food, tools, bedding, and other supplies. If the wagons were too heavy, they might get stuck. Then people would end up leaving supplies beside the trail.

Copy the story. Chunk it by marking the silent letters on your copy.

Imagine you were moving far

I

away and could take only one

a

plaything. What would you

p

take? Pioneer children had to

t

make this choice. They might

m

choose a book or a doll.

c

Families were supposed to pack

F

only what was needed.

o

1. Read the story to your student.

2. Read it together slowly. Have the student point to each word as you read.

3. Help your student find and mark the <u>**silent letters**</u> using orange.

Imagine you were moving far away and could take only one plaything. What would you take? Pioneer children had to make this choice. They might choose a book or a doll. Families were supposed to pack only what was needed. The wagons were filled with food, tools, bedding, and other supplies. If the wagons were too heavy, they might get stuck. Then people would end up leaving supplies beside the trail.

Copy the story. Chunk it by marking the silent letters on your copy.

The wagons were filled with

T

food, tools, bedding, and other

f

supplies. If the wagons were

s

too heavy, they might get

t

stuck. Then people would end

s

up leaving supplies beside

u

the trail.

t

1. Read the story to your student.

2. Read it together slowly. Have the student point to each word as you read.

3. Help your student find and mark the <u>**silent letters**</u> using orange.

Imagine you were moving far away and could take only one plaything. What would you take? Pioneer children had to make this choice. They might choose a book or a doll. Families were supposed to pack only what was needed. The wagons were filled with food, tools, bedding, and other supplies. If the wagons were too heavy, they might get stuck. Then people would end up leaving supplies beside the trail.

Copy the story. Chunk it by marking the silent letters on your copy.

Imagine you were moving far

I

away and could take only one

a

plaything. What would you

p

take? Pioneer children had to

t

make this choice. They might

m

choose a book or a doll.

c

Families were supposed to pack

F

only what was needed.

o

1. Read the story to your student.

2. Read it together slowly. Have the student point to each word as you read.

3. On 25D and 25E, you will look for common word endings. Together, find and mark the **endings** in pink or red.

Imagine you were moving far away and could take only one plaything. What would you take? Pioneer children had to make this choice. They might choose a book or a doll. Families were supposed to pack only what was needed. The wagons were filled with food, tools, bedding, and other supplies. If the wagons were too heavy, they might get stuck. Then people would end up leaving supplies beside the trail.

Endings
-ed -es -ful -ing -ly

Write this week's story from dictation. Ask for help if you need it.

Imagine

I spelled _____ words correctly.

1. Read the story to your student.

2. Read it together slowly. Have the student point to each word as you read.

3. Together, find and mark the <u>**endings**</u> in pink or red.

Imagine you were moving far away and could take only one plaything. What would you take? Pioneer children had to make this choice. They might choose a book or a doll. Families were supposed to pack only what was needed. The wagons were filled with food, tools, bedding, and other supplies. If the wagons were too heavy, they might get stuck. Then people would end up leaving supplies beside the trail.

Endings
-ed   -es   -ful   -ing   -ly

See if you can write this week's story from dictation without asking for help.

1. Read the story to your student.

2. Read it together slowly. Have the student point to each word as you read.

3. The letter *y* is often a consonant, but sometimes it is "tricky" and acts like a vowel. Together, look for **Tricky *y* Guy**. This *y* can be in the middle or at the end of a word. It may sound like long *e*, long *i*, or short *i*. Use green to mark <u>**Tricky *y* Guy**</u>.

Would you answer this ad? "Wanted: Young, skinny, wiry fellows not over 18. Must be expert riders willing to risk death daily." This was not a real ad for the Pony Express, but riders faced many dangers. They carried mail from Missouri to California. At stations along the way, the riders stopped to change horses. The Pony Express needed brave riders to carry the mail.

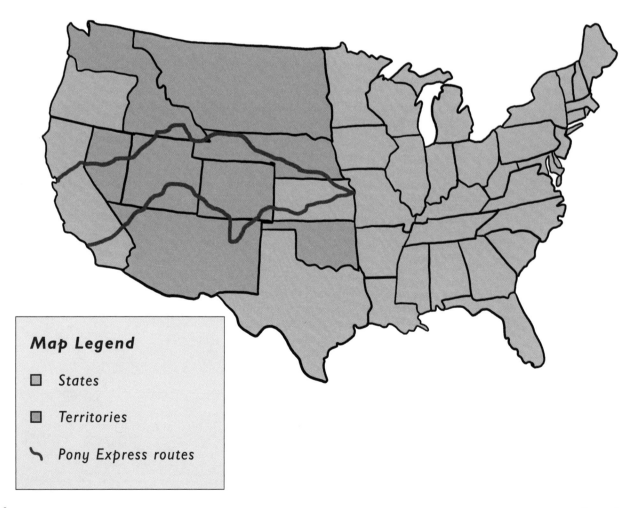

Map Legend

☐ States

☐ Territories

〰 Pony Express routes

Copy the story. Mark each Tricky *y* Guy on your copy.

Would you answer this ad?

W

"Wanted: Young, skinny, wiry

"W

fellows not over 18. Must be

f

expert riders willing to risk

e

death daily." This was not a

d

real ad for the Pony Express,

r

but riders faced many dangers.

b

1. Read the story to your student.

2. Read it together slowly. Have the student point to each word as you read.

3. Together, find and mark each **Tricky *y* Guy** in green.

Would you answer this ad? "Wanted: Young, skinny, wiry fellows not over 18. Must be expert riders willing to risk death daily." This was not a real ad for the Pony Express, but riders faced many dangers. They carried mail from Missouri to California. At stations along the way, the riders stopped to change horses. The Pony Express needed brave riders to carry the mail.

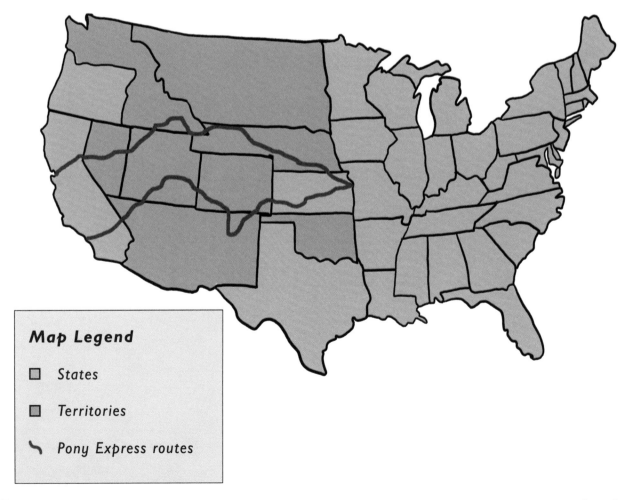

Map Legend

☐ *States*

☐ *Territories*

⟍ *Pony Express routes*

Copy the story. Mark each Tricky *y* Guy on your copy.

They carried mail from

T

Missouri to California. At

M

stations along the way, the

s

riders stopped to change

r

horses. The Pony Express

h

needed brave riders to carry

n

the mail.

t

1. Read the story to your student.

2. Read it together slowly. Have the student point to each word as you read.

3. Together, find and mark each **Tricky *y* Guy** in green.

Would you answer this ad? "Wanted: Young, skinny, wiry fellows not over 18. Must be expert riders willing to risk death daily." This was not a real ad for the Pony Express, but riders faced many dangers. They carried mail from Missouri to California. At stations along the way, the riders stopped to change horses. The Pony Express needed brave riders to carry the mail.

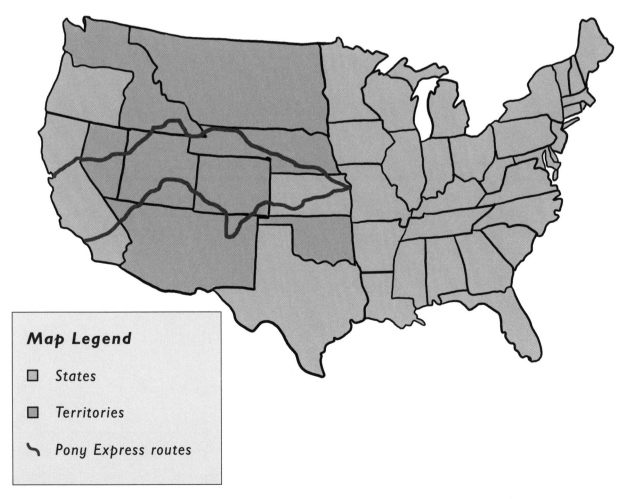

Map Legend

☐ States

☐ Territories

↘ Pony Express routes

Copy the story. Mark each Tricky *y* Guy on your copy.

Would you answer this ad?

W

"Wanted: Young, skinny, wiry

"W

fellows not over 18. Must be

f

expert riders willing to risk

e

death daily." This was not a

d

real ad for the Pony Express,

r

but riders faced many dangers.

b

1. Read the story to your student.

2. Read it together slowly. Have the student point to each word as you read.

3. On this page, find and mark the __endings__ in pink or red.

Would you answer this ad? "Wanted: Young, skinny, wiry fellows not over 18. Must be expert riders willing to risk death daily." This was not a real ad for the Pony Express, but riders faced many dangers. They carried mail from Missouri to California. At stations along the way, the riders stopped to change horses. The Pony Express needed brave riders to carry the mail.

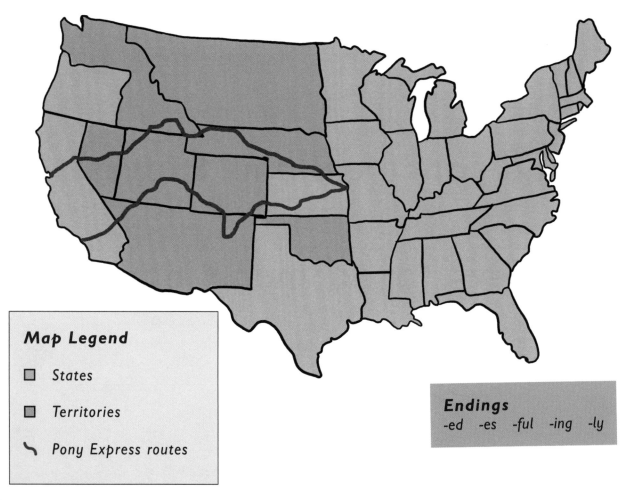

Map Legend

☐ States

☐ Territories

↳ Pony Express routes

Endings
-ed -es -ful -ing -ly

Write this week's story from dictation. Ask for help if you need it.

Would

26E

Section 1: Endings

1. Read the story to your student.

2. Read it together slowly. Have the student point to each word as you read.

3. Together, find and mark the <u>endings</u> in pink or red.

Would you answer this ad? "Wanted: Young, skinny, wiry fellows not over 18. Must be expert riders willing to risk death daily." This was not a real ad for the Pony Express, but riders faced many dangers. They carried mail from Missouri to California. At stations along the way, the riders stopped to change horses. The Pony Express needed brave riders to carry the mail.

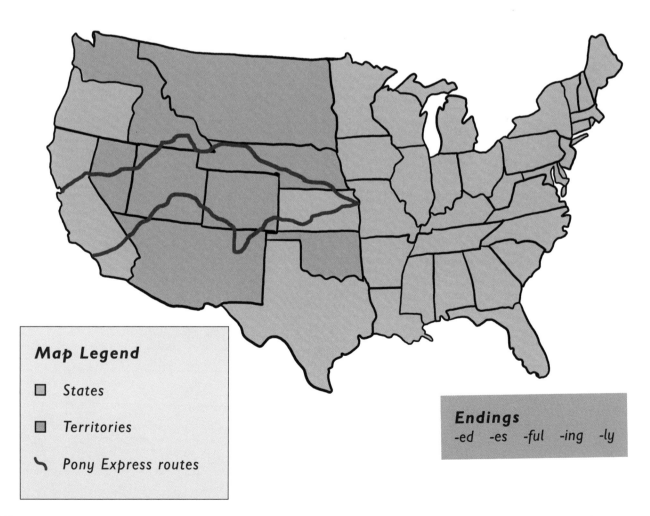

Map Legend

☐ States

◼ Territories

↖ Pony Express routes

Endings
-ed   -es   -ful   -ing   -ly

Section 2: Second Dictation

See if you can write this week's story from dictation without asking for help.

I spelled _____ words correctly.

1. Read the story to your student.

2. Read it together slowly. Have the student point to each word as you read.

3. Find and mark **Tricky *y* Guy** in green, <u>endings</u> in pink or red, and <u>silent letters</u> in orange. Don't forget the silent *l* in *walked* and the silent *h* in *Johnny*.

As a young man, Johnny Appleseed learned how to grow apple trees. When settlers moved into Ohio and Indiana, he planted orchards for them. He also planted orchards of his own and sold trees. Johnny lived simply. He had no house. He walked from place to place. His clothes were ragged. He is remembered for helping many needy people.

Endings
-ed -es -ful -ing -ly

Copy the story. Mark each Tricky *y* Guy, ending, and silent letter.

As a young man, Johnny

A

Appleseed learned how to grow

A

apple trees. When settlers

a

moved into Ohio and Indiana,

m

he planted orchards for them.

h

He also planted orchards of his

H

own and sold trees. Johnny

o

lived simply. He had no house.

l

1. Read the story to your student.

2. Read it together slowly. Have the student point to each word as you read.

3. Mark <u>**Tricky *y* Guy**</u> in green, <u>**endings**</u> in pink or red, and <u>**silent letters**</u> in orange.

As a young man, Johnny Appleseed learned how to grow apple trees. When settlers moved into Ohio and Indiana, he planted orchards for them. He also planted orchards of his own and sold trees. Johnny lived simply. He had no house. He walked from place to place. His clothes were ragged. He is remembered for helping many needy people.

Endings
-ed -es -ful -ing -ly

Copy the story. Mark each Tricky *y* Guy, ending, and silent letter.

He also planted orchards of his

H

own and sold trees. Johnny

o

lived simply. He had no house.

l

He walked from place to

H

place. His clothes were ragged.

p

He is remembered for helping

H

many needy people.

m

1. Read the story to your student.

2. Read it together slowly. Have the student point to each word as you read.

3. Mark **Tricky *y* Guy** in green, **endings** in pink or red, and **silent letters** in orange.

As a young man, Johnny Appleseed learned how to grow apple trees. When settlers moved into Ohio and Indiana, he planted orchards for them. He also planted orchards of his own and sold trees. Johnny lived simply. He had no house. He walked from place to place. His clothes were ragged. He is remembered for helping many needy people.

Endings
-ed -es -ful -ing -ly

Copy the story. Mark each Tricky *y* Guy, ending, and silent letter.

As a young man, Johnny

A

Appleseed learned how to grow

A

apple trees. When settlers

a

moved into Ohio and Indiana,

m

he planted orchards for them.

h

He also planted orchards of his

H

own and sold trees. Johnny

o

lived simply. He had no house.

l

1. Read the story to your student.

2. Read it together slowly. Have the student point to each word as you read.

3. Mark **Tricky *y* Guy** in green, **endings** in pink or red, and **silent letters** in orange.

As a young man, Johnny Appleseed learned how to grow apple trees. When settlers moved into Ohio and Indiana, he planted orchards for them. He also planted orchards of his own and sold trees. Johnny lived simply. He had no house. He walked from place to place. His clothes were ragged. He is remembered for helping many needy people.

Endings
-ed   -es   -ful   -ing   -ly

Section 2: First Dictation

Write this week's story from dictation. Ask for help if you need it.

As

1. Read the story to your student.

2. Read it together slowly. Have the student point to each word as you read.

3. Mark <u>**Tricky *y* Guy**</u> in green, <u>**endings**</u> in pink or red, and <u>**silent letters**</u> in orange.

As a young man, Johnny Appleseed learned how to grow apple trees. When settlers moved into Ohio and Indiana, he planted orchards for them. He also planted orchards of his own and sold trees. Johnny lived simply. He had no house. He walked from place to place. His clothes were ragged. He is remembered for helping many needy people.

Endings
-ed   -es   -ful   -ing   -ly

Section 2: Second Dictation

See if you can write this week's story from dictation without asking for help.

I spelled _____ words correctly.

1. Read the story to your student.

2. Read it together slowly. Have the student point to each word as you read.

3. This week you and your student will be marking all six letter patterns that you have learned. They are **vowel chunks** (yellow), **consonant chunks** (blue), **Bossy _r_ chunks** (purple), **Tricky _y_ Guy** (green), **endings** (pink or red), and **silent letters** (orange). (Note: The word _view_ has overlapping vowel chunks. You may choose whichever one you prefer.)

Katharine Bates took a train ride across the country. She saw many beautiful sights. In Colorado she went to the top of Pikes Peak. She was over a mile above the city below. She could see so far that the distant mountains looked purple. The beautiful view gave her great joy. Back in her hotel, she put her thoughts into a poem. It became the song "America, the Beautiful."

Endings
-ed -es -ful -ing -ly

Vowel Chunks
aa ae ai ao au aw ay
ea ee ei eo ew ey eau
ia ie ii io iu
oa oe oi oo ou ow oy
ua ue ui uo uy

Consonant Chunks
ch gh ph sh th wh
gn kn qu wr dg ck tch
bb cc dd ff gg hh kk ll mm
nn pp rr ss tt ww vv zz

Bossy r Chunks
ar er ir or ur

Copy and chunk the story. Mark all the letter patterns you have learned.

Katharine Bates took a train

K

ride across the country. She

r

saw many beautiful sights. In

s

Colorado she went to the top

C

of Pikes Peak. She was over a

o

mile above the city below.

m

She could see so far that the

S

distant mountains looked purple.

d

1. Read the story to your student.

2. Read it together slowly. Have the student point to each word as you read.

3. Help your student mark the <u>**vowel chunks**</u> (yellow), <u>**consonant chunks**</u> (blue), <u>**Bossy *r* chunks**</u> (purple), <u>**Tricky *y* Guy**</u> (green), <u>**endings**</u> (pink or red), and <u>**silent letters**</u> (orange).

Katharine Bates took a train ride across the country. She saw many beautiful sights. In Colorado she went to the top of Pikes Peak. She was over a mile above the city below. She could see so far that the distant mountains looked purple. The beautiful view gave her great joy. Back in her hotel, she put her thoughts into a poem. It became the song "America, the Beautiful."

Endings

-ed   -es   -ful   -ing   -ly

Vowel Chunks

aa   ae   ai   ao   au   aw   ay

ea   ee   ei   eo   ew   ey   eau

ia   ie   ii   io   iu

oa   oe   oi   oo   ou   ow   oy

ua   ue   ui   uo   uy

Consonant Chunks

ch   gh   ph   sh   th   wh

gn   kn   qu   wr   dg   ck   tch

bb   cc   dd   ff   gg   hh   kk   ll   mm

nn   pp   rr   ss   tt   ww   vv   zz

Bossy r Chunks

ar   er   ir   or   ur

Copy and chunk the story. Mark all the letter patterns you have learned.

She could see so far that the
s

distant mountains looked purple.
d

The beautiful view gave her
T

great joy. Back in her hotel,
g

she put her thoughts into a
s

poem. It became the song
p

"America, the Beautiful."
"A

1. Read the story to your student.

2. Read it together slowly. Have the student point to each word as you read.

3. Help your student mark the <u>vowel chunks</u> (yellow), <u>consonant chunks</u> (blue), <u>**Bossy *r* chunks**</u> (purple), <u>**Tricky *y* Guy**</u> (green), <u>endings</u> (pink or red), and <u>silent letters</u> (orange).

Katharine Bates took a train ride across the country. She saw many beautiful sights. In Colorado she went to the top of Pikes Peak. She was over a mile above the city below. She could see so far that the distant mountains looked purple. The beautiful view gave her great joy. Back in her hotel, she put her thoughts into a poem. It became the song "America, the Beautiful."

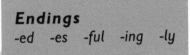

Endings
-ed -es -ful -ing -ly

Vowel Chunks
aa ae ai ao au aw ay
ea ee ei eo ew ey eau
ia ie ii io iu
oa oe oi oo ou ow oy
ua ue ui uo uy

Consonant Chunks
ch gh ph sh th wh
gn kn qu wr dg ck tch
bb cc dd ff gg hh kk ll mm
nn pp rr ss tt ww vv zz

Bossy r Chunks
ar er ir or ur

Copy and chunk the story. Mark all the letter patterns you have learned.

Katharine Bates took a train

K

ride across the country. She

r

saw many beautiful sights. In

s

Colorado she went to the top

C

of Pikes Peak. She was over a

o

mile above the city below.

m

She could see so far that the

S

distant mountains looked purple.

d

1. Read the story to your student.

2. Read it together slowly. Have the student point to each word as you read.

3. Help your student mark the **vowel chunks** (yellow), **consonant chunks** (blue), **Bossy _r_ chunks** (purple), **Tricky _y_ Guy** (green), **endings** (pink or red), and **silent letters** (orange).

Katharine Bates took a train ride across the country. She saw many beautiful sights. In Colorado she went to the top of Pikes Peak. She was over a mile above the city below. She could see so far that the distant mountains looked purple. The beautiful view gave her great joy. Back in her hotel, she put her thoughts into a poem. It became the song "America, the Beautiful."

Endings
-ed -es -ful -ing -ly

Vowel Chunks
aa ae ai ao au aw ay
ea ee ei eo ew ey eau
ia ie ii io iu
oa oe oi oo ou ow oy
ua ue ui uo uy

Consonant Chunks
ch gh ph sh th wh
gn kn qu wr dg ck tch
bb cc dd ff gg hh kk ll mm
nn pp rr ss tt ww vv zz

Bossy r Chunks
ar er ir or ur

Write this week's story from dictation. Ask for help if you need it.

Katharine

1. Read the story to your student.

2. Read it together slowly. Have the student point to each word as you read.

3. Help your student mark the <u>**vowel chunks**</u> (yellow), <u>**consonant chunks**</u> (blue), <u>**Bossy *r* chunks**</u> (purple), <u>**Tricky *y* Guy**</u> (green), <u>**endings**</u> (pink or red), and <u>**silent letters**</u> (orange).

Katharine Bates took a train ride across the country. She saw many beautiful sights. In Colorado she went to the top of Pikes Peak. She was over a mile above the city below. She could see so far that the distant mountains looked purple. The beautiful view gave her great joy. Back in her hotel, she put her thoughts into a poem. It became the song "America, the Beautiful."

Endings
-ed   -es   -ful   -ing   -ly

Vowel Chunks
aa   ae   ai   ao   au   aw   ay
ea   ee   ei   eo   ew   ey   eau
ia   ie   ii   io   iu
oa   oe   oi   oo   ou   ow   oy
ua   ue   ui   uo   uy

Consonant Chunks
ch   gh   ph   sh   th   wh
gn   kn   qu   wr   dg   ck   tch
bb   cc   dd   ff   gg   hh   kk   ll   mm
nn   pp   rr   ss   tt   ww   vv   zz

Bossy r Chunks
ar   er   ir   or   ur

Section 2: Second Dictation

See if you can write this week's story from dictation without asking for help.

1. Read the story to your student.

2. Read it together slowly. Have the student point to each word as you read.

3. This week you and your student will be marking all six letter patterns. They are **vowel chunks** (yellow), **consonant chunks** (blue), **Bossy *r* chunks** (purple), **Tricky *y* Guy** (green), **endings** (pink or red), and **silent letters** (orange). (Note: It is suggested that you mark the ending rather than the vowel chunk in *being*.)

President Theodore Roosevelt loved being outdoors. He hiked and hunted. He believed that America needed to guard its wild places. He set aside land for five national parks and 150 national forests. He also saved 51 places where birds gather when they fly south for the winter. Maybe you can visit one of these beautiful, wild places.

Consonant Chunks

ch	gh	ph	sh	th	wh		
gn	kn	qu	wr	dg	ck	tch	
bb	cc	dd	ff	gg	hh	kk	ll	mm
nn	pp	rr	ss	tt	ww	vv	zz

Endings

-ed   -es   -ful   -ing   -ly

Bossy r Chunks

ar   er   ir   or   ur

Vowel Chunks

aa	ae	ai	ao	au	aw	ay
ea	ee	ei	eo	ew	ey	eau
ia	ie	ii	io	iu		
oa	oe	oi	oo	ou	ow	oy
ua	ue	ui	uo	uy		

Section 2: Copywork

Copy and chunk the story. Mark all the letter patterns you have learned.

President Theodore Roosevelt

P

loved being outdoors. He

l

hiked and hunted. He believed

h

that America needed to guard

t

its wild places. He set aside

i

land for five national parks

l

and 150 national forests.

a

Americana **29A**

105

29B

1. Read the story to your student.

2. Read it together slowly. Have the student point to each word as you read.

3. Mark the **vowel chunks** (yellow), **consonant chunks** (blue), **Bossy r chunks** (purple), **Tricky _y_ Guy** (green), **endings** (pink or red), and **silent letters** (orange).

President Theodore Roosevelt loved being outdoors. He hiked and hunted. He believed that America needed to guard its wild places. He set aside land for five national parks and 150 national forests. He also saved 51 places where birds gather when they fly south for the winter. Maybe you can visit one of these beautiful, wild places.

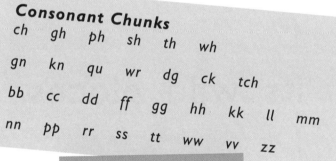

Consonant Chunks

ch	gh	ph	sh	th	wh			
gn	kn	qu	wr	dg	ck	tch		
bb	cc	dd	ff	gg	hh	kk	ll	mm
nn	pp	rr	ss	tt	ww	vv	zz	

Endings
-ed -es -ful -ing -ly

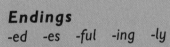

Bossy r Chunks
ar   er   ir   or   ur

Vowel Chunks

aa	ae	ai	ao	au	aw	ay
ea	ee	ei	eo	ew	ey	eau
ia	ie	ii	io	iu		
oa	oe	oi	oo	ou	ow	oy
ua	ue	ui	uo	uy		

Copy and chunk the story. Mark all the letter patterns you have learned.

He set aside land for five

H

national parks and 150

n

national forests. He also

n

saved 51 places where birds

s

gather when they fly south

g

for the winter. Maybe you can

f

visit one of these beautiful,

v

wild places.

w

1. Read the story to your student.

2. Read it together slowly. Have the student point to each word as you read.

3. Mark the <u>**vowel chunks**</u> (yellow), <u>**consonant chunks**</u> (blue), <u>**Bossy *r* chunks**</u> (purple), <u>**Tricky *y* Guy**</u> (green), <u>**endings**</u> (pink or red), and <u>**silent letters**</u> (orange).

President Theodore Roosevelt loved being outdoors. He hiked and hunted. He believed that America needed to guard its wild places. He set aside land for five national parks and 150 national forests. He also saved 51 places where birds gather when they fly south for the winter. Maybe you can visit one of these beautiful, wild places.

Consonant Chunks

ch   gh   ph   sh   th   wh
gn   kn   qu   wr   dg   ck   tch
bb   cc   dd   ff   gg   hh   kk   ll   mm
nn   pp   rr   ss   tt   ww   vv   zz

Endings
-ed   -es   -ful   -ing   -ly

Bossy r Chunks
ar   er   ir   or   ur

Vowel Chunks
aa   ae   ai   ao   au   aw   ay
ea   ee   ei   eo   ew   ey   eau
ia   ie   ii   io   iu
oa   oe   oi   oo   ou   ow   oy
ua   ue   ui   uo   uy

Copy and chunk the story. Mark all the letter patterns you have learned.

President Theodore Roosevelt

P

loved being outdoors. He

l

hiked and hunted. He believed

h

that America needed to guard

t

its wild places. He set aside

i

land for five national parks

l

and 150 national forests.

a

1. Read the story to your student.

2. Read it together slowly. Have the student point to each word as you read.

3. Mark the **vowel chunks** (yellow), **consonant chunks** (blue), **Bossy r chunks** (purple), **Tricky *y* Guy** (green), **endings** (pink or red), and **silent letters** (orange).

President Theodore Roosevelt loved being outdoors. He hiked and hunted. He believed that America needed to guard its wild places. He set aside land for five national parks and 150 national forests. He also saved 51 places where birds gather when they fly south for the winter. Maybe you can visit one of these beautiful, wild places.

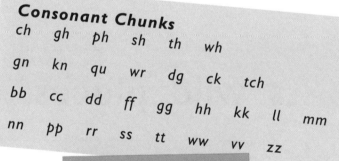

Consonant Chunks

ch	gh	ph	sh	th	wh			
gn	kn	qu	wr	dg	ck	tch		
bb	cc	dd	ff	gg	hh	kk	ll	mm
nn	pp	rr	ss	tt	ww	vv	zz	

Endings
-ed -es -ful -ing -ly

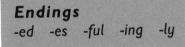

Bossy r Chunks
ar   er   ir   or   ur

Vowel Chunks

aa	ae	ai	ao	au	aw	ay
ea	ee	ei	eo	ew	ey	eau
ia	ie	ii	io	iu		
oa	oe	oi	oo	ou	ow	oy
ua	ue	ui	uo	uy		

Write this week's story from dictation. Ask for help if you need it.

President

1. Read the story to your student.

2. Read it together slowly. Have the student point to each word as you read.

3. Mark the **vowel chunks** (yellow), **consonant chunks** (blue), **Bossy *r* chunks** (purple), **Tricky *y* Guy** (green), **endings** (pink or red), and **silent letters** (orange).

President Theodore Roosevelt loved being outdoors. He hiked and hunted. He believed that America needed to guard its wild places. He set aside land for five national parks and 150 national forests. He also saved 51 places where birds gather when they fly south for the winter. Maybe you can visit one of these beautiful, wild places.

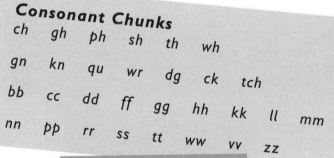

Consonant Chunks

ch	gh	ph	sh	th	wh			
gn	kn	qu	wr	dg	ck	tch		
bb	cc	dd	ff	gg	hh	kk	ll	mm
nn	pp	rr	ss	tt	ww	vv	zz	

Endings
-ed -es -ful -ing -ly

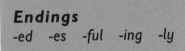

Bossy r Chunks
ar   er   ir   or   ur

Vowel Chunks

aa	ae	ai	ao	au	aw	ay
ea	ee	ei	eo	ew	ey	eau
ia	ie	ii	io	iu		
oa	oe	oi	oo	ou	ow	oy
ua	ue	ui	uo	uy		

Section 2: Second Dictation

See if you can write this week's story from dictation without asking for help.

1. Read the story to your student.

2. Read it together slowly. Have the student point to each word as you read.

3. This week you and your student will be marking all six letter patterns. They are <u>vowel chunks</u> (yellow), <u>consonant chunks</u> (blue), <u>Bossy *r* chunks</u> (purple), <u>Tricky *y* Guy</u> (green), <u>endings</u> (pink or red), and <u>silent letters</u> (orange).

On the side of a stone cliff, 400 workers blasted and drilled. They etched and hammered. They sanded and smoothed. They worked and sweated for many years. On the side of Mount Rushmore, they carved the faces of four great presidents! Each face is as tall as a six-story building. If you ever go to South Dakota, stop and see this huge carving.

Consonant Chunks

ch	gh	ph	sh	th	wh			
gn	kn	qu	wr	dg	ck	tch		
bb	cc	dd	ff	gg	hh	kk	ll	mm
nn	pp	rr	ss	tt	ww	vv	zz	

Vowel Chunks

aa	ae	ai	ao	au	aw	ay
ea	ee	ei	eo	ew	ey	eau
ia	ie	ii	io	iu		
oa	oe	oi	oo	ou	ow	oy
ua	ue	ui	uo	uy		

Bossy r Chunks

ar er ir or ur

Endings

-ed -es -ful -ing -ly

Copy and chunk the story. Mark all the letter patterns you have learned.

On the side of a stone cliff,

O

400 workers blasted and drilled.

4

They etched and hammered.

T

They sanded and smoothed.

T

They worked and sweated for

T

many years. On the side of

m

Mount Rushmore, they carved

M

the faces of four great presidents!

t

1. Read the story to your student.

2. Read it together slowly. Have the student point to each word as you read.

3. Mark the **vowel chunks** (yellow), **consonant chunks** (blue), **Bossy *r* chunks** (purple), **Tricky *y* Guy** (green), **endings** (pink or red), and **silent letters** (orange).

On the side of a stone cliff, 400 workers blasted and drilled. They etched and hammered. They sanded and smoothed. They worked and sweated for many years. On the side of Mount Rushmore, they carved the faces of four great presidents! Each face is as tall as a six-story building. If you ever go to South Dakota, stop and see this huge carving.

Consonant Chunks

ch	gh	ph	sh	th	wh
gn	kn	qu	wr	dg	ck	tch
bb	cc	dd	ff	gg	hh	kk	ll	mm
nn	pp	rr	ss	tt	ww	vv	zz

Vowel Chunks

aa	ae	ai	ao	au	aw	ay
ea	ee	ei	eo	ew	ey	eau
ia	ie	ii	io	iu
oa	oe	oi	oo	ou	ow	oy
ua	ue	ui	uo	uy

Bossy r Chunks

ar er ir or ur

Endings

-ed -es -ful -ing -ly

Copy and chunk the story. Mark all the letter patterns you have learned.

On the side of Mount

O

Rushmore, they carved the

R

faces of four great presidents!

f

Each face is as tall as a

E

six-story building. If you ever

s

go to South Dakota, stop and

g

see this huge carving.

s

1. Read the story to your student.

2. Read it together slowly. Have the student point to each word as you read.

3. Mark the **vowel chunks** (yellow), **consonant chunks** (blue), **Bossy r chunks** (purple), **Tricky _y_ Guy** (green), **endings** (pink or red), and **silent letters** (orange).

On the side of a stone cliff, 400 workers blasted and drilled. They etched and hammered. They sanded and smoothed. They worked and sweated for many years. On the side of Mount Rushmore, they carved the faces of four great presidents! Each face is as tall as a six-story building. If you ever go to South Dakota, stop and see this huge carving.

Consonant Chunks

ch   gh   ph   sh   th   wh

gn   kn   qu   wr   dg   ck   tch

bb   cc   dd   ff   gg   hh   kk   ll   mm

nn   pp   rr   ss   tt   ww   vv   zz

Vowel Chunks

aa   ae   ai   ao   au   aw   ay

ea   ee   ei   eo   ew   ey   eau

ia   ie   ii   io   iu

oa   oe   oi   oo   ou   ow   oy

ua   ue   ui   uo   uy

Bossy r Chunks

ar   er   ir   or   ur

Endings

-ed   -es   -ful   -ing   -ly

Copy and chunk the story. Mark all the letter patterns you have learned.

They etched and hammered.

T

They sanded and smoothed.

T

They worked and sweated

T

for many years. On the side

f

# of Mount Rushmore, they

o

carved the faces of four great

c

presidents!

p

1. Read the story to your student.

2. Read it together slowly. Have the student point to each word as you read.

3. Mark the **vowel chunks** (yellow), **consonant chunks** (blue), **Bossy *r* chunks** (purple), **Tricky *y* Guy** (green), **endings** (pink or red), and **silent letters** (orange).

On the side of a stone cliff, 400 workers blasted and drilled. They etched and hammered. They sanded and smoothed. They worked and sweated for many years. On the side of Mount Rushmore, they carved the faces of four great presidents! Each face is as tall as a six-story building. If you ever go to South Dakota, stop and see this huge carving.

Consonant Chunks

ch	gh	ph	sh	th	wh	
gn	kn	qu	wr	dg	ck	tch
bb	cc	dd	ff	gg	hh	kk	ll	mm
nn	pp	rr	ss	tt	ww	vv	zz

Vowel Chunks

aa	ae	ai	ao	au	aw	ay
ea	ee	ei	eo	ew	ey	eau
ia	ie	ii	io	iu		
oa	oe	oi	oo	ou	ow	oy
ua	ue	ui	uo	uy		

Bossy r Chunks

ar   er   ir   or   ur

Endings

-ed   -es   -ful   -ing   -ly

Section 2: First Dictation

Write this week's story from dictation. Ask for help if you need it.

On

1. Read the story to your student.

2. Read it together slowly. Have the student point to each word as you read.

3. Mark the <u>**vowel chunks**</u> (yellow), <u>**consonant chunks**</u> (blue), <u>**Bossy *r* chunks**</u> (purple), <u>**Tricky *y* Guy**</u> (green), <u>**endings**</u> (pink or red), and <u>**silent letters**</u> (orange).

On the side of a stone cliff, 400 workers blasted and drilled. They etched and hammered. They sanded and smoothed. They worked and sweated for many years. On the side of Mount Rushmore, they carved the faces of four great presidents! Each face is as tall as a six-story building. If you ever go to South Dakota, stop and see this huge carving.

Consonant Chunks

ch	gh	ph	sh	th	wh		
gn	kn	qu	wr	dg	ck	tch	
bb	cc	dd	ff	gg	hh	kk	ll	mm
nn	pp	rr	ss	tt	ww	vv	zz

Vowel Chunks

aa	ae	ai	ao	au	aw	ay
ea	ee	ei	eo	ew	ey	eau
ia	ie	ii	io	iu		
oa	oe	oi	oo	ou	ow	oy
ua	ue	ui	uo	uy		

Bossy r Chunks

ar er ir or ur

Endings

-ed -es -ful -ing -ly

Section 2: Second Dictation

See if you can write this week's story from dictation without asking for help.

1. Read the story to your student.

2. Read it together slowly. Have the student point to each word as you read.

3. Mark the **vowel chunks** (yellow), **consonant chunks** (blue), **Bossy _r_ chunks** (purple), **Tricky _y_ Guy** (green), **endings** (pink or red), and **silent letters** (orange).

Looking down into the water, James couldn't believe his eyes.
Was that gold? He picked up some flakes and took them to
his boss, John Sutter. Together they tested the tiny flakes.
They had found real gold! At first John tried to keep it a secret.
Soon news spread, and the Gold Rush was on. People came
to California, hoping to get rich. Some did. Most did not.
But many people stayed and settled California.

Consonant Chunks

ch	gh	ph	sh	th	wh
gn	kn	qu	wr	dg	ck	tch
bb	cc	dd	ff	gg	hh	kk	ll	mm
nn	pp	rr	ss	tt	ww	vv	zz

Vowel Chunks

aa	ae	ai	ao	au	aw	ay
ea	ee	ei	eo	ew	ey	eau
ia	ie	ii	io	iu
oa	oe	oi	oo	ou	ow	oy
ua	ue	ui	uo	uy

Bossy r Chunks

ar   er   ir   or   ur

Endings
-ed -es -ful -ing -ly

Copy and chunk the story. Mark all the letter patterns you have learned.

Looking down into the water,

L

James couldn't believe his eyes.

J

Was that gold? He picked up

W

some flakes and took them to

s

his boss, John Sutter. Together

h

they tested the tiny flakes.

t

They had found real gold!

T

1. Read the story to your student.

2. Read it together slowly. Have the student point to each word as you read.

3. Mark the <u>**vowel chunks**</u> (yellow), <u>**consonant chunks**</u> (blue), <u>**Bossy *r* chunks**</u> (purple), <u>**Tricky *y* Guy**</u> (green), <u>**endings**</u> (pink or red), and <u>**silent letters**</u> (orange).

Looking down into the water, James couldn't believe his eyes.
Was that gold? He picked up some flakes and took them to
his boss, John Sutter. Together they tested the tiny flakes.
They had found real gold! At first John tried to keep it a secret.
Soon news spread, and the Gold Rush was on. People came
to California, hoping to get rich. Some did. Most did not.
But many people stayed and settled California.

Consonant Chunks

ch   gh   ph   sh   th   wh
gn   kn   qu   wr   dg   ck   tch
bb   cc   dd   ff   gg   hh   kk   ll   mm
nn   pp   rr   ss   tt   ww   vv   zz

Vowel Chunks

aa   ae   ai   ao   au   aw   ay
ea   ee   ei   eo   ew   ey   eau
ia   ie   ii   io   iu
oa   oe   oi   oo   ou   ow   oy
ua   ue   ui   uo   uy

Bossy r Chunks

ar   er   ir   or   ur

Endings

-ed   -es   -ful   -ing   -ly

Copy and chunk the story. Mark all the letter patterns you have learned.

At first John tried to keep it a

A

secret. Soon news spread, and

s

the Gold Rush was on. People

t

came to California, hoping to

c

get rich. Some did. Most did

g

not. But many people stayed

n

and settled California.

a

1. Read the story to your student.

2. Read it together slowly. Have the student point to each word as you read.

3. Mark the **vowel chunks** (yellow), **consonant chunks** (blue), **Bossy _r_ chunks** (purple), **Tricky _y_ Guy** (green), **endings** (pink or red), and **silent letters** (orange).

Looking down into the water, James couldn't believe his eyes. Was that gold? He picked up some flakes and took them to his boss, John Sutter. Together they tested the tiny flakes. They had found real gold! At first John tried to keep it a secret. Soon news spread, and the Gold Rush was on. People came to California, hoping to get rich. Some did. Most did not. But many people stayed and settled California.

Consonant Chunks

ch	gh	ph	sh	th	wh			
gn	kn	qu	wr	dg	ck	tch		
bb	cc	dd	ff	gg	hh	kk	ll	mm
nn	pp	rr	ss	tt	ww	vv	zz	

Vowel Chunks

aa	ae	ai	ao	au	aw	ay
ea	ee	ei	eo	ew	ey	eau
ia	ie	ii	io	iu		
oa	oe	oi	oo	ou	ow	oy
ua	ue	ui	uo	uy		

Bossy r Chunks

ar er ir or ur

Endings

-ed -es -ful -ing -ly

Section 2: Copywork

Copy and chunk the story. Mark all the letter patterns you have learned.

Looking down into the water,

L

James couldn't believe his eyes.

J

Was that gold? He picked up

W

some flakes and took them to

s

his boss, John Sutter. Together

h

they tested the tiny flakes.

t

They had found real gold!

T

1. Read the story to your student.

2. Read it together slowly. Have the student point to each word as you read.

3. Mark the <u>vowel chunks</u> (yellow), <u>consonant chunks</u> (blue), <u>**Bossy r chunks**</u> (purple), <u>**Tricky y Guy**</u> (green), <u>endings</u> (pink or red), and <u>silent letters</u> (orange).

Looking down into the water, James couldn't believe his eyes. Was that gold? He picked up some flakes and took them to his boss, John Sutter. Together they tested the tiny flakes. They had found real gold! At first John tried to keep it a secret. Soon news spread, and the Gold Rush was on. People came to California, hoping to get rich. Some did. Most did not. But many people stayed and settled California.

Consonant Chunks

ch	gh	ph	sh	th	wh			
gn	kn	qu	wr	dg	ck	tch		
bb	cc	dd	ff	gg	hh	kk	ll	mm
nn	pp	rr	ss	tt	ww	vv	zz	

Vowel Chunks

aa	ae	ai	ao	au	aw	ay
ea	ee	ei	eo	ew	ey	eau
ia	ie	ii	io	iu		
oa	oe	oi	oo	ou	ow	oy
ua	ue	ui	uo	uy		

Bossy r Chunks

ar   er   ir   or   ur

Endings

-ed   -es   -ful   -ing   -ly

Write this week's story from dictation. Ask for help if you need it.

Looking

1. Read the story to your student.

2. Read it together slowly. Have the student point to each word as you read.

3. Mark the **vowel chunks** (yellow), **consonant chunks** (blue), **Bossy *r* chunks** (purple), **Tricky *y* Guy** (green), **endings** (pink or red), and **silent letters** (orange).

Looking down into the water, James couldn't believe his eyes.
Was that gold? He picked up some flakes and took them to
his boss, John Sutter. Together they tested the tiny flakes.
They had found real gold! At first John tried to keep it a secret.
Soon news spread, and the Gold Rush was on. People came
to California, hoping to get rich. Some did. Most did not.
But many people stayed and settled California.

Consonant Chunks

ch	gh	ph	sh	th	wh
gn	kn	qu	wr	dg	ck	tch
bb	cc	dd	ff	gg	hh	kk	ll	mm
nn	pp	rr	ss	tt	ww	vv	zz

Vowel Chunks

aa	ae	ai	ao	au	aw	ay
ea	ee	ei	eo	ew	ey	eau
ia	ie	ii	io	iu
oa	oe	oi	oo	ou	ow	oy
ua	ue	ui	uo	uy

Bossy r Chunks

ar   er   ir   or   ur

Endings

-ed   -es   -ful   -ing   -ly

Section 2: Second Dictation

See if you can write this week's story from dictation without asking for help.

1. Read the story to your student.

2. Read it together slowly. Have the student point to each word as you read.

3. Mark the **vowel chunks** (yellow), **consonant chunks** (blue), **Bossy _r_ chunks** (purple), **Tricky _y_ Guy** (green), **endings** (pink or red), and **silent letters** (orange).

Americans love reading tall tales about Paul Bunyan. The stories aren't true, but many people think they are funny. Here is one. When Paul was born, he was a giant. He slept in a lumber wagon. Soon he grew too big for the wagon. Then his parents built a huge raft, and he slept on the ocean. If he turned over in his sleep, he made waves big enough to sink ships.

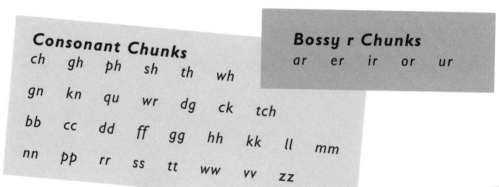

Consonant Chunks

ch   gh   ph   sh   th   wh

gn   kn   qu   wr   dg   ck   tch

bb   cc   dd   ff   gg   hh   kk   ll   mm

nn   pp   rr   ss   tt   ww   vv   zz

Bossy r Chunks

ar   er   ir   or   ur

Vowel Chunks

aa   ae   ai   ao   au   aw   ay

ea   ee   ei   eo   ew   ey   eau

ia   ie   ii   io   iu

oa   oe   oi   oo   ou   ow   oy

ua   ue   ui   uo   uy

Endings

-ed   -es   -ful   -ing   -ly

Copy and chunk the story. Mark all the letter patterns you have learned.

Americans love reading tall

A

tales about Paul Bunyan. The

t

stories aren't true, but many

s

people think they are funny.

P

Here is one. When Paul was

H

born, he was a giant. He slept

b

in a lumber wagon. Soon he

i

grew too big for the wagon.

g

1. Read the story to your student.

2. Read it together slowly. Have the student point to each word as you read.

3. Mark the <u>vowel chunks</u> (yellow), <u>consonant chunks</u> (blue), <u>**Bossy *r* chunks**</u> (purple), <u>**Tricky *y* Guy**</u> (green), <u>endings</u> (pink or red), and <u>silent letters</u> (orange).

Americans love reading tall tales about Paul Bunyan. The stories aren't true, but many people think they are funny. Here is one. When Paul was born, he was a giant. He slept in a lumber wagon. Soon he grew too big for the wagon. Then his parents built a huge raft, and he slept on the ocean. If he turned over in his sleep, he made waves big enough to sink ships.

Consonant Chunks

ch gh ph sh th wh

gn kn qu wr dg ck tch

bb cc dd ff gg hh kk ll mm

nn pp rr ss tt ww vv zz

Bossy r Chunks

ar er ir or ur

Vowel Chunks

aa ae ai ao au aw ay

ea ee ei eo ew ey eau

ia ie ii io iu

oa oe oi oo ou ow oy

ua ue ui uo uy

Endings

-ed -es -ful -ing -ly

Copy and chunk the story. Mark all the letter patterns you have learned.

He slept in a lumber wagon.

H

Soon he grew too big for the

S

wagon. Then his parents built

w

a huge raft, and he slept on

a

the ocean. If he turned over

t

in his sleep, he made waves

i

big enough to sink ships.

b

1. Read the story to your student.

2. Read it together slowly. Have the student point to each word as you read.

3. Mark the <u>vowel chunks</u> (yellow), <u>consonant chunks</u> (blue), <u>Bossy *r* chunks</u> (purple), <u>Tricky *y* Guy</u> (green), <u>endings</u> (pink or red), and <u>silent letters</u> (orange).

Americans love reading tall tales about Paul Bunyan. The stories aren't true, but many people think they are funny. Here is one. When Paul was born, he was a giant. He slept in a lumber wagon. Soon he grew too big for the wagon. Then his parents built a huge raft, and he slept on the ocean. If he turned over in his sleep, he made waves big enough to sink ships.

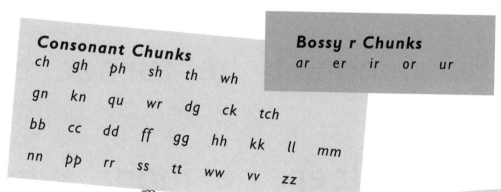

Consonant Chunks

ch gh ph sh th wh
gn kn qu wr dg ck tch
bb cc dd ff gg hh kk ll mm
nn pp rr ss tt ww vv zz

Bossy r Chunks

ar er ir or ur

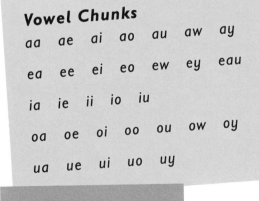

Vowel Chunks

aa ae ai ao au aw ay
ea ee ei eo ew ey eau
ia ie ii io iu
oa oe oi oo ou ow oy
ua ue ui uo uy

Endings

-ed -es -ful -ing -ly

Copy and chunk the story. Mark all the letter patterns you have learned.

Americans love reading tall

A

tales about Paul Bunyan. The

t

stories aren't true, but many

s

people think they are funny.

P

Here is one. When Paul was

H

born, he was a giant. He slept

b

in a lumber wagon. Soon he

i

grew too big for the wagon.

g

1. Read the story to your student.

2. Read it together slowly. Have the student point to each word as you read.

3. Mark the **vowel chunks** (yellow), **consonant chunks** (blue), **Bossy _r_ chunks** (purple), **Tricky _y_ Guy** (green), **endings** (pink or red), and **silent letters** (orange).

Americans love reading tall tales about Paul Bunyan. The stories aren't true, but many people think they are funny. Here is one. When Paul was born, he was a giant. He slept in a lumber wagon. Soon he grew too big for the wagon. Then his parents built a huge raft, and he slept on the ocean. If he turned over in his sleep, he made waves big enough to sink ships.

Consonant Chunks

ch gh ph sh th wh
gn kn qu wr dg ck tch
bb cc dd ff gg hh kk ll mm
nn pp rr ss tt ww vv zz

Bossy r Chunks

ar er ir or ur

Vowel Chunks

aa ae ai ao au aw ay
ea ee ei eo ew ey eau
ia ie ii io iu
oa oe oi oo ou ow oy
ua ue ui uo uy

Endings

-ed -es -ful -ing -ly

Write this week's story from dictation. And ask for help if you need it.

Americans

1. Read the story to your student.

2. Read it together slowly. Have the student point to each word as you read.

3. Mark the <u>vowel chunks</u> (yellow), <u>consonant chunks</u> (blue), <u>**Bossy *r* chunks**</u> (purple), <u>**Tricky *y* Guy**</u> (green), <u>endings</u> (pink or red), and <u>silent letters</u> (orange).

Americans love reading tall tales about Paul Bunyan. The stories aren't true, but many people think they are funny. Here is one. When Paul was born, he was a giant. He slept in a lumber wagon. Soon he grew too big for the wagon. Then his parents built a huge raft, and he slept on the ocean. If he turned over in his sleep, he made waves big enough to sink ships.

Consonant Chunks

ch   gh   ph   sh   th   wh
gn   kn   qu   wr   dg   ck   tch
bb   cc   dd   ff   gg   hh   kk   ll   mm
nn   pp   rr   ss   tt   ww   vv   zz

Bossy r Chunks

ar   er   ir   or   ur

Vowel Chunks

aa   ae   ai   ao   au   aw   ay
ea   ee   ei   eo   ew   ey   eau
ia   ie   ii   io   iu
oa   oe   oi   oo   ou   ow   oy
ua   ue   ui   uo   uy

Endings

-ed   -es   -ful   -ing   -ly

Section 2: Second Dictation

See if you can write this week's story from dictation without asking for help.

I spelled _____ words correctly.

1. Read the story to your student.

2. Read it together slowly. Have the student point to each word as you read.

3. Together, mark the <u>vowel chunks</u>, <u>consonant chunks</u>, <u>**Bossy *r* chunks**</u>, <u>**Tricky *y* Guy**</u>, <u>endings</u>, and <u>silent letters</u>, using the correct colors for each. Refer to your ***Instructor's Handbook*** if you need help.

As a young man, Samuel Clemens worked as a steamboat pilot on the Mississippi River. When the boat was in water twelve feet deep, Clemens would hear someone call out, "By the mark twain!" Later in life, he was writing short stories and wanted to use a pen name. Mark Twain was a perfect name. He used this name when he wrote his famous stories about Tom Sawyer and Huck Finn.

Vowel Chunks

aa	ae	ai	ao	au	aw	ay
ea	ee	ei	eo	ew	ey	eau
ia	ie	ii	io	iu		
oa	oe	oi	oo	ou	ow	oy
ua	ue	ui	uo	uy		

Bossy r Chunks

ar   er   ir   or   ur

Endings

-ed   -es   -ful   -ing   -ly

Consonant Chunks

ch	gh	ph	sh	th	wh	
gn	kn	qu	wr	dg	ck	tch
bb	cc	dd	ff	gg	hh	kk	ll	mm
nn	pp	rr	ss	tt	ww	vv	zz

Section 2: Copywork

Copy and chunk the story. Mark all the letter patterns you have learned.

As a young man, Samuel

A

Clemens worked as a

C

steamboat pilot on the

s

Mississippi River. When the boat

M

was in water twelve feet deep,

w

Clemens would hear someone

C

call out, "By the mark twain!"

C

1. Read the story to your student.

2. Read it together slowly. Have the student point to each word as you read.

3. Together, mark the <u>vowel chunks</u>, <u>consonant chunks</u>, <u>Bossy *r* chunks</u>, <u>Tricky *y* Guy</u>, <u>endings</u>, and <u>silent letters</u>, using the correct colors for each.

As a young man, Samuel Clemens worked as a steamboat pilot on the Mississippi River. When the boat was in water twelve feet deep, Clemens would hear someone call out, "By the mark twain!" Later in life, he was writing short stories and wanted to use a pen name. Mark Twain was a perfect name. He used this name when he wrote his famous stories about Tom Sawyer and Huck Finn.

Vowel Chunks

aa   ae   ai   ao   au   aw   ay

ea   ee   ei   eo   ew   ey   eau

ia   ie   ii   io   iu

oa   oe   oi   oo   ou   ow   oy

ua   ue   ui   uo   uy

Bossy r Chunks

ar   er   ir   or   ur

Endings

-ed   -es   -ful   -ing   -ly

Consonant Chunks

ch   gh   ph   sh   th   wh

gn   kn   qu   wr   dg   ck   tch

bb   cc   dd   ff   gg   hh   kk   ll   mm

nn   pp   rr   ss   tt   ww   vv   zz

Copy and chunk the story. Mark all the letter patterns you have learned.

Later in life, he was writing

L

short stories and wanted to

s

use a pen name. Mark Twain

u

was a perfect name. He used

w

this name when he wrote his

t

famous stories about Tom

f

Sawyer and Huck Finn.

S

1. Read the story to your student.

2. Read it together slowly. Have the student point to each word as you read.

3. Together, mark the **vowel chunks**, **consonant chunks**, **Bossy *r* chunks**, **Tricky *y* Guy**, **endings**, and **silent letters**, using the correct colors for each.

As a young man, Samuel Clemens worked as a steamboat pilot on the Mississippi River. When the boat was in water twelve feet deep, Clemens would hear someone call out, "By the mark twain!" Later in life, he was writing short stories and wanted to use a pen name. Mark Twain was a perfect name. He used this name when he wrote his famous stories about Tom Sawyer and Huck Finn.

Vowel Chunks

aa ae ai ao au aw ay

ea ee ei eo ew ey eau

ia ie ii io iu

oa oe oi oo ou ow oy

ua ue ui uo uy

Bossy r Chunks

ar er ir or ur

Endings

-ed -es -ful -ing -ly

Consonant Chunks

ch gh ph sh th wh

gn kn qu wr dg ck tch

bb cc dd ff gg hh kk ll mm

nn pp rr ss tt ww vv zz

Copy and chunk the story. Mark all the letter patterns you have learned.

As a young man, Samuel

A

Clemens worked as a

C

steamboat pilot on the

s

Mississippi River. When the boat

M

was in water twelve feet deep,

W

Clemens would hear someone

C

call out, "By the mark twain!"

C

33D

Section 1: All Letter Patterns

1. Read the story to your student.

2. Read it together slowly. Have the student point to each word as you read.

3. Together, mark the **vowel chunks**, **consonant chunks**, **Bossy _r_ chunks**, **Tricky _y_ Guy**, **endings**, and **silent letters**, using the correct colors for each.

As a young man, Samuel Clemens worked as a steamboat pilot on the Mississippi River. When the boat was in water twelve feet deep, Clemens would hear someone call out, "By the mark twain!" Later in life, he was writing short stories and wanted to use a pen name. Mark Twain was a perfect name. He used this name when he wrote his famous stories about Tom Sawyer and Huck Finn.

Vowel Chunks

aa	ae	ai	ao	au	aw	ay
ea	ee	ei	eo	ew	ey	eau
ia	ie	ii	io	iu		
oa	oe	oi	oo	ou	ow	oy
ua	ue	ui	uo	uy		

Bossy r Chunks

ar   er   ir   or   ur

Endings

-ed   -es   -ful   -ing   -ly

Consonant Chunks

ch	gh	ph	sh	th	wh	
gn	kn	qu	wr	dg	ck	tch
bb	cc	dd	ff	gg	hh	kk	ll	mm
nn	pp	rr	ss	tt	ww	vv	zz

Section 2: First Dictation

Write this week's story from dictation. Ask for help if you need it.

As

I spelled _____ words correctly.

1. Read the story to your student.

2. Read it together slowly. Have the student point to each word as you read.

3. Together, mark the <u>vowel chunks</u>, <u>consonant chunks</u>, <u>Bossy *r* chunks</u>, <u>Tricky *y* Guy</u>, <u>endings</u>, and <u>silent letters</u>, using the correct colors for each.

As a young man, Samuel Clemens worked as a steamboat pilot on the Mississippi River. When the boat was in water twelve feet deep, Clemens would hear someone call out, "By the mark twain!" Later in life, he was writing short stories and wanted to use a pen name. Mark Twain was a perfect name. He used this name when he wrote his famous stories about Tom Sawyer and Huck Finn.

Vowel Chunks

aa	ae	ai	ao	au	aw	ay
ea	ee	ei	eo	ew	ey	eau
ia	ie	ii	io	iu		
oa	oe	oi	oo	ou	ow	oy
ua	ue	ui	uo	uy		

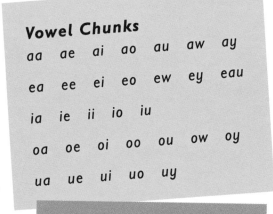

Bossy r Chunks

ar   er   ir   or   ur

Endings

-ed -es -ful -ing -ly

Consonant Chunks

ch	gh	ph	sh	th	wh			
gn	kn	qu	wr	dg	ck	tch		
bb	cc	dd	ff	gg	hh	kk	ll	mm
nn	pp	rr	ss	tt	ww	vv	zz	

Section 2: Second Dictation

See if you can write this week's story from dictation without asking for help.

I spelled _____ words correctly.

1. Read the story to your student.

2. Read it together slowly. Have the student point to each word as you read.

3. Together, mark the <u>vowel chunks</u>, <u>consonant chunks</u>, <u>Bossy *r* chunks</u>, <u>Tricky *y* Guy</u>, <u>endings</u>, and <u>silent letters</u>, using the correct colors for each.

Eleanor was the wife of President Franklin D. Roosevelt. As First Lady, she did more than host parties. She worked to make life better for people. She gave speeches and raised money. She helped the young and the poor. She gave jobs to women and African Americans. She visited soldiers during World War 2. Someone said, "She would rather light a candle than curse the darkness."

Consonant Chunks

ch	gh	ph	sh	th	wh			
gn	kn	qu	wr	dg	ck	tch		
bb	cc	dd	ff	gg	hh	kk	ll	mm
nn	pp	rr	ss	tt	ww	vv	zz	

Vowel Chunks

aa	ae	ai	ao	au	aw	ay
ea	ee	ei	eo	ew	ey	eau
ia	ie	ii	io	iu		
oa	oe	oi	oo	ou	ow	oy
ua	ue	ui	uo	uy		

Bossy r Chunks

ar   er   ir   or   ur

Endings

-ed   -es   -ful   -ing   -ly

Copy and chunk the story. Mark all the letter patterns you have learned.

Eleanor was the wife of

E

President Franklin D. Roosevelt.

P

As First Lady, she did more

A

than host parties. She worked

t

to make life better for people.

t

She gave speeches and raised

S

money. She helped the young

m

and the poor.

a

1. Read the story to your student.

2. Read it together slowly. Have the student point to each word as you read.

3. Together, mark the **vowel chunks**, **consonant chunks**, **Bossy r chunks**, **Tricky *y* Guy**, **endings**, and **silent letters**, using the correct colors for each.

Eleanor was the wife of President Franklin D. Roosevelt. As First Lady, she did more than host parties. She worked to make life better for people. She gave speeches and raised money. She helped the young and the poor. She gave jobs to women and African Americans. She visited soldiers during World War 2. Someone said, "She would rather light a candle than curse the darkness."

Consonant Chunks

ch   gh   ph   sh   th   wh

gn   kn   qu   wr   dg   ck   tch

bb   cc   dd   ff   gg   hh   kk   ll   mm

nn   pp   rr   ss   tt   ww   vv   zz

Vowel Chunks

aa   ae   ai   ao   au   aw   ay

ea   ee   ei   eo   ew   ey   eau

ia   ie   ii   io   iu

oa   oe   oi   oo   ou   ow   oy

ua   ue   ui   uo   uy

Bossy r Chunks

ar   er   ir   or   ur

Endings

-ed   -es   -ful   -ing   -ly

Copy and chunk the story. Mark all the letter patterns you have learned.

She helped the young and the

S

poor. She gave jobs to women

p

and African Americans. She

a

visited soldiers during World

v

War 2. Someone said, "She

W

would rather light a candle

w

than curse the darkness."

t

1. Read the story to your student.

2. Read it together slowly. Have the student point to each word as you read.

3. Together, mark the **vowel chunks**, **consonant chunks**, **Bossy r chunks**, **Tricky *y* Guy**, **endings**, and **silent letters**, using the correct colors for each.

Eleanor was the wife of President Franklin D. Roosevelt. As First Lady, she did more than host parties. She worked to make life better for people. She gave speeches and raised money. She helped the young and the poor. She gave jobs to women and African Americans. She visited soldiers during World War 2. Someone said, "She would rather light a candle than curse the darkness."

Consonant Chunks

ch	gh	ph	sh	th	wh
gn	kn	qu	wr	dg	ck	tch
bb	cc	dd	ff	gg	hh	kk	ll	mm
nn	pp	rr	ss	tt	ww	vv	zz

Vowel Chunks

aa ae ai ao au aw ay

ea ee ei eo ew ey eau

ia ie ii io iu

oa oe oi oo ou ow oy

ua ue ui uo uy

Bossy r Chunks

ar er ir or ur

Endings

-ed -es -ful -ing -ly

Section 2: Copywork

Copy and chunk the story. Mark all the letter patterns you have learned.

Eleanor was the wife of

E

President Franklin D. Roosevelt.

P

As First Lady, she did more

A

than host parties. She worked

t

to make life better for people.

t

She gave speeches and raised

S

money. She helped the young

m

and the poor.

a

1. Read the story to your student.

2. Read it together slowly. Have the student point to each word as you read.

3. Together, mark the **vowel chunks**, **consonant chunks**, **Bossy *r* chunks**, **Tricky *y* Guy**, **endings**, and **silent letters**, using the correct colors for each.

Eleanor was the wife of President Franklin D. Roosevelt. As First Lady, she did more than host parties. She worked to make life better for people. She gave speeches and raised money. She helped the young and the poor. She gave jobs to women and African Americans. She visited soldiers during World War 2. Someone said, "She would rather light a candle than curse the darkness."

Consonant Chunks

ch	gh	ph	sh	th	wh			
gn	kn	qu	wr	dg	ck	tch		
bb	cc	dd	ff	gg	hh	kk	ll	mm
nn	pp	rr	ss	tt	ww	vv	zz	

Vowel Chunks

aa	ae	ai	ao	au	aw	ay
ea	ee	ei	eo	ew	ey	eau
ia	ie	ii	io	iu		
oa	oe	oi	oo	ou	ow	oy
ua	ue	ui	uo	uy		

Bossy r Chunks

ar   er   ir   or   ur

Endings

-ed   -es   -ful   -ing   -ly

Write this week's story from dictation. Take your time and ask for help if you need it.

Eleanor

1. Read the story to your student.

2. Read it together slowly. Have the student point to each word as you read.

3. Together, mark the <u>vowel chunks</u>, <u>consonant chunks</u>, <u>Bossy *r* chunks</u>, <u>Tricky *y* Guy</u>, <u>endings</u>, and <u>silent letters</u>, using the correct colors for each.

Eleanor was the wife of President Franklin D. Roosevelt. As First Lady, she did more than host parties. She worked to make life better for people. She gave speeches and raised money. She helped the young and the poor. She gave jobs to women and African Americans. She visited soldiers during World War 2. Someone said, "She would rather light a candle than curse the darkness."

Consonant Chunks

ch gh ph sh th wh
gn kn qu wr dg ck tch
bb cc dd ff gg hh kk ll mm
nn pp rr ss tt ww vv zz

Vowel Chunks

aa ae ai ao au aw ay
ea ee ei eo ew ey eau
ia ie ii io iu
oa oe oi oo ou ow oy
ua ue ui uo uy

Bossy r Chunks

ar er ir or ur

Endings

-ed -es -ful -ing -ly

Section 2: Second Dictation

See if you can write this week's story from dictation without asking for help.

1. Read the story to your student.

2. Read it together slowly. Have the student point to each word as you read.

3. Mark **vowel chunks**, **consonant chunks**, **Bossy *r* chunks**, **Tricky *y* Guy**, **endings**, and **silent letters**. Look carefully for the silent *l* and the silent *b*.
   (Note: The brackets around the word *a* indicate that it is unclear what Armstrong actually said. Your student does not need to include the brackets in the copywork or dictation.)

The spacecraft landed carefully. There was nothing around for miles and miles. There were only rocks, soil, craters, and outer space. A man climbed out of the hatch and down the ladder. As he stepped onto the soft, gray soil, he said, "That's one small step for [a] man, one giant leap for mankind." This was quite a moment in history. Neil Armstrong was the first person to walk on the moon!

Endings
-ed -es -ful -ing -ly

Consonant Chunks

ch	gh	ph	sh	th	wh		
gn	kn	qu	wr	dg	ck	tch	
bb	cc	dd	ff	gg	hh	kk	ll	mm
nn	pp	rr	ss	tt	ww	vv	zz

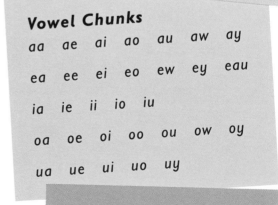

Vowel Chunks

aa	ae	ai	ao	au	aw	ay
ea	ee	ei	eo	ew	ey	eau
ia	ie	ii	io	iu		
oa	oe	oi	oo	ou	ow	oy
ua	ue	ui	uo	uy		

Bossy r Chunks

ar er ir or ur

Copy and chunk the story. Mark all the letter patterns you have learned.

The spacecraft landed carefully.

T

There was nothing around

T

for miles and miles. There were

f

only rocks, soil, craters, and

o

outer space. A man climbed

o

out of the hatch and down

o

the ladder.

t

35B

Section 1: All Letter Patterns

1. Read the story to your student.

2. Read it together slowly. Have the student point to each word as you read.

3. Together, mark the <u>vowel chunks</u>, <u>consonant chunks</u>, <u>Bossy *r* chunks</u>, <u>Tricky *y* Guy</u>, <u>endings</u>, and <u>silent letters</u>, using the correct colors for each.

The spacecraft landed carefully. There was nothing around for miles and miles. There were only rocks, soil, craters, and outer space. A man climbed out of the hatch and down the ladder. As he stepped onto the soft, gray soil, he said, "That's one small step for [a] man, one giant leap for mankind." This was quite a moment in history. Neil Armstrong was the first person to walk on the moon!

Endings

-ed   -es   -ful   -ing   -ly

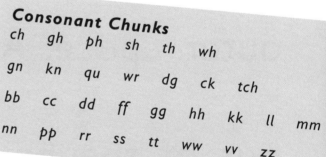

Consonant Chunks

ch   gh   ph   sh   th   wh

gn   kn   qu   wr   dg   ck   tch

bb   cc   dd   ff   gg   hh   kk   ll   mm

nn   pp   rr   ss   tt   ww   vv   zz

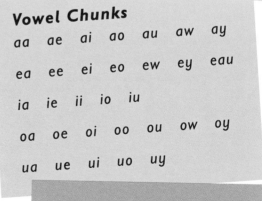

Vowel Chunks

aa   ae   ai   ao   au   aw   ay

ea   ee   ei   eo   ew   ey   eau

ia   ie   ii   io   iu

oa   oe   oi   oo   ou   ow   oy

ua   ue   ui   uo   uy

Bossy r Chunks

ar   er   ir   or   ur

Copy and chunk the story. Mark all the letter patterns you have learned.

As he stepped onto the soft,

A

gray soil, he said, "That's one

g

small step for a man, one

s

giant leap for mankind." This

g

was quite a moment in history.

w

Neil Armstrong was the first

N

person to walk on the moon!

P

1. Read the story to your student.

2. Read it together slowly. Have the student point to each word as you read.

3. Together, mark the <u>vowel chunks</u>, <u>consonant chunks</u>, <u>**Bossy *r* chunks**</u>, <u>Tricky *y* Guy</u>, <u>endings</u>, and <u>silent letters</u>, using the correct colors for each.

The spacecraft landed carefully. There was nothing around for miles and miles. There were only rocks, soil, craters, and outer space. A man climbed out of the hatch and down the ladder. As he stepped onto the soft, gray soil, he said, "That's one small step for [a] man, one giant leap for mankind." This was quite a moment in history. Neil Armstrong was the first person to walk on the moon!

Endings

-ed   -es   -ful   -ing   -ly

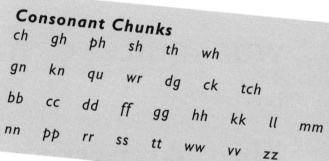

Consonant Chunks

ch	gh	ph	sh	th	wh	
gn	kn	qu	wr	dg	ck	tch
bb	cc	dd	ff	gg	hh	kk	ll	mm
nn	pp	rr	ss	tt	ww	vv	zz

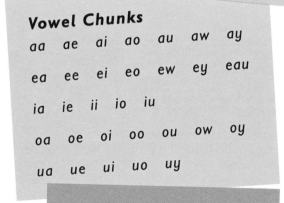

Vowel Chunks

aa	ae	ai	ao	au	aw	ay
ea	ee	ei	eo	ew	ey	eau
ia	ie	ii	io	iu		
oa	oe	oi	oo	ou	ow	oy
ua	ue	ui	uo	uy		

Bossy r Chunks

ar   er   ir   or   ur

Copy and chunk the story. Mark all the letter patterns you have learned.

The spacecraft landed carefully.

T

There was nothing around

T

for miles and miles. There were

f

only rocks, soil, craters, and

o

outer space. A man climbed

o

out of the hatch and down

o

the ladder.

t

1. Read the story to your student.

2. Read it together slowly. Have the student point to each word as you read.

3. Together, mark the <u>**vowel chunks**</u>, <u>**consonant chunks**</u>, <u>**Bossy _r_ chunks**</u>, <u>**Tricky _y_ Guy**</u>, <u>**endings**</u>, and <u>**silent letters**</u>, using the correct colors for each.

The spacecraft landed carefully. There was nothing around for miles and miles. There were only rocks, soil, craters, and outer space. A man climbed out of the hatch and down the ladder. As he stepped onto the soft, gray soil, he said, "That's one small step for [a] man, one giant leap for mankind." This was quite a moment in history. Neil Armstrong was the first person to walk on the moon!

Endings
-ed -es -ful -ing -ly

Consonant Chunks

ch	gh	ph	sh	th	wh		
gn	kn	qu	wr	dg	ck	tch	
bb	cc	dd	ff	gg	hh	kk	ll	mm
nn	pp	rr	ss	tt	ww	vv	zz

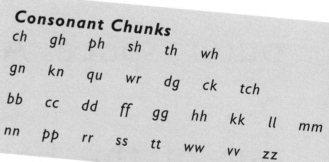

Vowel Chunks

aa	ae	ai	ao	au	aw	ay
ea	ee	ei	eo	ew	ey	eau
ia	ie	ii	io	iu		
oa	oe	oi	oo	ou	ow	oy
ua	ue	ui	uo	uy		

Bossy r Chunks
ar   er   ir   or   ur

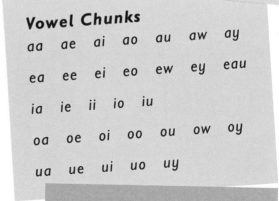

Write this week's story from dictation. Ask for help if you need it.

The

I spelled _____ words correctly.

1. Read the story to your student.

2. Read it together slowly. Have the student point to each word as you read.

3. Together, mark the **vowel chunks**, **consonant chunks**, **Bossy r chunks**, **Tricky *y* Guy**, **endings**, and **silent letters**, using the correct colors for each.

The spacecraft landed carefully. There was nothing around for miles and miles. There were only rocks, soil, craters, and outer space. A man climbed out of the hatch and down the ladder. As he stepped onto the soft, gray soil, he said, "That's one small step for [a] man, one giant leap for mankind." This was quite a moment in history. Neil Armstrong was the first person to walk on the moon!

Endings
-ed -es -ful -ing -ly

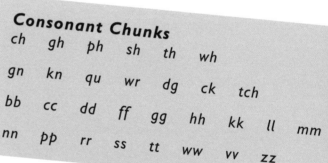

Consonant Chunks
ch gh ph sh th wh
gn kn qu wr dg ck tch
bb cc dd ff gg hh kk ll mm
nn pp rr ss tt ww vv zz

Vowel Chunks
aa ae ai ao au aw ay
ea ee ei eo ew ey eau
ia ie ii io iu
oa oe oi oo ou ow oy
ua ue ui uo uy

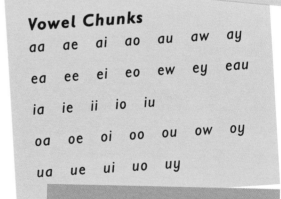

Bossy r Chunks
ar er ir or ur

Section 2: Second Dictation

See if you can write this week's story from dictation without asking for help.

I spelled _____ words correctly.

1. Read the story to your student.

2. Read it together slowly. Have the student point to each word as you read.

3. Together, mark the **vowel chunks**, **consonant chunks**, **Bossy *r* chunks**, **Tricky *y* Guy**, **endings**, and **silent letters**, using the correct colors for each.

Levi Strauss and his family came to America. They started several stores. During the Gold Rush, Levi headed west. He wasn't looking for gold in the ground like other people were. He wanted to sell things like cloth, clothing, and bedding. Twenty years later, a tailor asked Levi to help him. The man wanted to make sturdy denim overalls. Their first denim jeans were made in the 1890s.

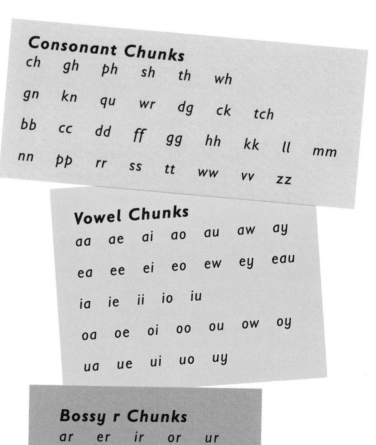

Consonant Chunks

ch gh ph sh th wh
gn kn qu wr dg ck tch
bb cc dd ff gg hh kk ll mm
nn pp rr ss tt ww vv zz

Vowel Chunks

aa ae ai ao au aw ay
ea ee ei eo ew ey eau
ia ie ii io iu
oa oe oi oo ou ow oy
ua ue ui uo uy

Bossy r Chunks

ar er ir or ur

Endings

-ed -es -ful -ing -ly

Copy and chunk the story. Mark all the letter patterns you have learned.

Levi Strauss and his family

L

came to America. They started

c

several stores. During the Gold

s

Rush, Levi headed west. He

R

wasn't looking for gold in the

w

ground like other people were.

g

He wanted to sell things like

H

cloth, clothing, and bedding.

c

1. Read the story to your student.

2. Read it together slowly. Have the student point to each word as you read.

3. Together, mark the <u>vowel chunks</u>, <u>consonant chunks</u>, <u>Bossy *r* chunks</u>, Tricky *y* Guy, <u>endings</u>, and <u>silent letters</u>, using the correct colors for each.

Levi Strauss and his family came to America. They started several stores. During the Gold Rush, Levi headed west. He wasn't looking for gold in the ground like other people were. He wanted to sell things like cloth, clothing, and bedding. Twenty years later, a tailor asked Levi to help him. The man wanted to make sturdy denim overalls. Their first denim jeans were made in the 1890s.

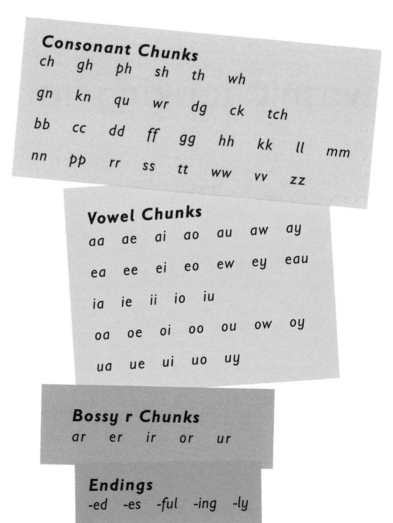

Consonant Chunks

ch gh ph sh th wh

gn kn qu wr dg ck tch

bb cc dd ff gg hh kk ll mm

nn pp rr ss tt ww vv zz

Vowel Chunks

aa ae ai ao au aw ay

ea ee ei eo ew ey eau

ia ie ii io iu

oa oe oi oo ou ow oy

ua ue ui uo uy

Bossy r Chunks

ar er ir or ur

Endings

-ed -es -ful -ing -ly

Copy and chunk the story. Mark all the letter patterns you have learned.

He wanted to sell things like

H

cloth, clothing, and bedding.

c

Twenty years later, a tailor

T

asked Levi to help him. The

a

man wanted to make sturdy

m

denim overalls. Their first denim

d

jeans were made in the 1890s.

j

1. Read the story to your student.

2. Read it together slowly. Have the student point to each word as you read.

3. Together, mark the <u>**vowel chunks**</u>, <u>**consonant chunks**</u>, <u>**Bossy *r* chunks**</u>, <u>**Tricky *y* Guy**</u>, <u>**endings**</u>, and <u>**silent letters**</u>, using the correct colors for each.

Levi Strauss and his family came to America. They started several stores. During the Gold Rush, Levi headed west. He wasn't looking for gold in the ground like other people were. He wanted to sell things like cloth, clothing, and bedding. Twenty years later, a tailor asked Levi to help him. The man wanted to make sturdy denim overalls. Their first denim jeans were made in the 1890s.

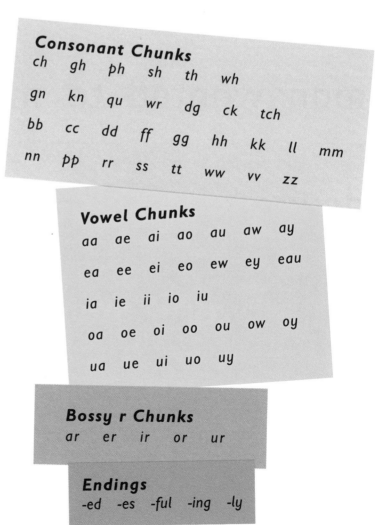

Consonant Chunks

ch   gh   ph   sh   th   wh
gn   kn   qu   wr   dg   ck   tch
bb   cc   dd   ff   gg   hh   kk   ll   mm
nn   pp   rr   ss   tt   ww   vv   zz

Vowel Chunks

aa   ae   ai   ao   au   aw   ay
ea   ee   ei   eo   ew   ey   eau
ia   ie   ii   io   iu
oa   oe   oi   oo   ou   ow   oy
ua   ue   ui   uo   uy

Bossy r Chunks

ar   er   ir   or   ur

Endings

-ed   -es   -ful   -ing   -ly

Copy and chunk the story. Mark all the letter patterns you have learned.

Levi Strauss and his family

L

came to America. They started

c

several stores. During the Gold

s

Rush, Levi headed west. He

R

wasn't looking for gold in the

w

ground like other people were.

g

He wanted to sell things like

H

cloth, clothing, and bedding.

c

1. Read the story to your student.

2. Read it together slowly. Have the student point to each word as you read.

3. Together, mark the <u>vowel chunks</u>, <u>consonant chunks</u>, <u>Bossy *r* chunks</u>, <u>Tricky *y* Guy</u>, <u>endings</u>, and <u>silent letters</u>, using the correct colors for each.

Levi Strauss and his family came to America. They started several stores. During the Gold Rush, Levi headed west. He wasn't looking for gold in the ground like other people were. He wanted to sell things like cloth, clothing, and bedding. Twenty years later, a tailor asked Levi to help him. The man wanted to make sturdy denim overalls. Their first denim jeans were made in the 1890s.

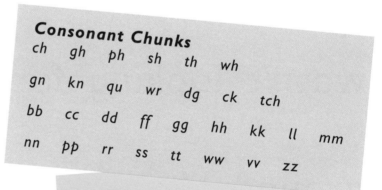

Consonant Chunks

ch	gh	ph	sh	th	wh	
gn	kn	qu	wr	dg	ck	tch
bb	cc	dd	ff	gg	hh	kk	ll	mm
nn	pp	rr	ss	tt	ww	vv	zz

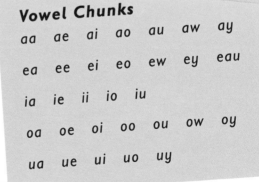

Vowel Chunks

aa	ae	ai	ao	au	aw	ay
ea	ee	ei	eo	ew	ey	eau
ia	ie	ii	io	iu
oa	oe	oi	oo	ou	ow	oy
ua	ue	ui	uo	uy

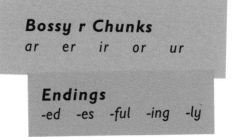

Bossy r Chunks

ar   er   ir   or   ur

Endings

-ed   -es   -ful   -ing   -ly

Section 2: First Dictation

Write this week's story from dictation. Ask for help if you need it.

Levi

I spelled _____ words correctly.

36E

1. Read the story to your student.

2. Read it together slowly. Have the student point to each word as you read.

3. Together, mark the <u>vowel chunks</u>, <u>consonant chunks</u>, <u>Bossy *r* chunks</u>, <u>Tricky *y* Guy</u>, <u>endings</u>, and <u>silent letters</u>, using the correct colors for each.

Levi Strauss and his family came to America. They started several stores. During the Gold Rush, Levi headed west. He wasn't looking for gold in the ground like other people were. He wanted to sell things like cloth, clothing, and bedding. Twenty years later, a tailor asked Levi to help him. The man wanted to make sturdy denim overalls. Their first denim jeans were made in the 1890s.

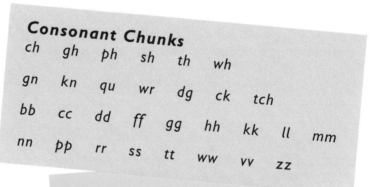

Consonant Chunks

ch gh ph sh th wh
gn kn qu wr dg ck tch
bb cc dd ff gg hh kk ll mm
nn pp rr ss tt ww vv zz

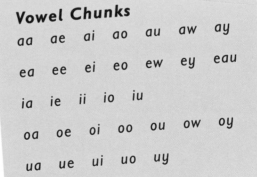

Vowel Chunks

aa ae ai ao au aw ay
ea ee ei eo ew ey eau
ia ie ii io iu
oa oe oi oo ou ow oy
ua ue ui uo uy

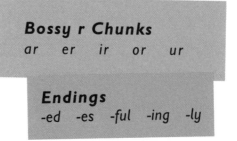

Bossy r Chunks

ar er ir or ur

Endings

-ed -es -ful -ing -ly